Falco Tarassaco
Oberto Airaudi

THE SYNCHRONIC LINES

The energy streams of planet Earth

Falco Tarassaco (Oberto Airaudi)
THE SYNCHRONIC LINES
The energy streams of Planet Earth
Edited by Elefantina Genziana (Alma Foà)

ISBN: 978-88-99652-30-2

Devodama Srl, Vidracco (TO), Italy
Copyright 2015© by DEVODAMA

First Edition - June 2015

Cover: Selfic Painting by Oberto Airaudi
Title:"An indicator of stellar highways and vital Synchronic Lines, selective of species carrying souls in planetary transit ..." 01/2004

CONTENTS

PRESENTATION

(Dicembre 1998)

H ere we have an idea that underlies so many cul-
tures, both spiritual and naturalistic: the idea
that this planet is in many ways like a living being. In Synchronic Lines Falco Tarassaco, Oberto Airaudi[1],
the founder and spiritual guide of the Community of
Damanhur, takes this further and suggests that the Earth
is in contact with other living worlds, and joined ultimately with the entire Universe.

This has been an essential part of the author's teach-
ing from the beginning.

Writing as early as 1980, in his book "Sincronicità e
Linee Sincroniche"[2], (Synchronicity and the Synchronic
Lines) Falco Tarassaco described the existence of a universal network, an immense web uniting all worlds
where there was life in the widest sense of the word.
A network which spreads out over the face of the Earth
in a network of eighteen principle lines and countless
secondary ones.

The system of synchronic lines represents, as Falco
depicts it, at one and the same time the nervous system of the planet, its sensory apparatus, and its inner
senses – the functions which in the case of individuals

5

too, allow us to receive stimuli from the outer and the inner realms and bring them together in an expansion of consciousness.

When the original book came out, the comparison that seemed most apt at the time, was to liken the Synchronic Lines to autostrade – to highways with traffic flowing in both directions, passing through toll points regulating the flow, and fed by traffic coming in from minor roads.

Thirty years on, our minds turn irresistibly to the internet, because of the universality of the contact that it provides and because of its highly articulated structure with information cirulating along underground cables, through the ether or even in "clouds". The Synchronic Lines similarly travel through the air, snake through the earth under our feet, and execute arabesques as they cross the continents (yet, unaccountably, never following coastlines).

The present volume faithfully reflects Falco's thought – which earlier than 1980 was already being published regularly in the monthly magazine Notiziario Horus[3]– and densely explained in his lessons on spiritual physics, gathered together and put in order by Damanhurian researchers passionately interested in the subject, for the 1998 edition.

These days, quantum physics makes it increasingly clear that the gap between spiritual and scientific visions (the latter not confined to "science") is destined to narrow to nothing.

6

Sooner or later, as with the Copernican Revolution when it was no longer possible to escape the evidence that the Earth revolved around the Sun, the day will come when all will accept that the Universe is a great thought, crisscrossed by the principle functions that thought performs: life and communication.

Until that day comes our time would best be devoted to research and development. This volume – a tale shaped by the author, and a blank sheet for readers to fill with their own hypotheses – is an exciting starting point. In line with the spirit of research in Damanhur, Falco proposes hypotheses, to then be developed by so many theses.

7

Elefantina Genziana (Alma Foà)

[1] Falco Tarassaco - Oberto Airaudi (Balangero, Turin - 29 May 1950 - Cuceglio, Turin - 23 June 2013).

[2] Oberto Airaudi, *Le Linee Sincroniche del pianeta Terra (The Synchronic Lines of Planet Earth)*, appeared in instalments between 1981 and 1982, in *Horus Newsletter* (see Note 3) supplemented by *Sincronicità e Linee Sincroniche (Synchronicity and the Synchronic Lines)* published Horus, Turin, 1985, followed by other editions, to date.

[3] *The Notiziario Horus (Horus Newsletter)* was the original informative magazine, published between1975 and 1987 from the Horus centre in Turin. It dealt with topics such as natural medicine, esotericism and paranormal phenomena. From 1985 onward it became the organ of information for the Federation of Damanhur, aimed primarily at centres in Italy and the rest of Europe.

PREFACE

THE THEORY OF SYNCHRONICITY

Before immersing ourselves in the extraordinary subject of *The Synchronic Lines of planet Earth*, an introductory overview of the concepts discussed in *sincronicità*, and a brief review of the main theories of modern physics, should prove useful in helping us to better understand and enter more fully into this subject.

The western world, which sees Man as a reasoning and rational being, has always found it difficult to swallow that there could be any such thing as *synchronicity*. But, if we deny this concept, how is it possible to justify or explain away, those events that we have all experienced in the course of our lives, which occur apparently "coincidentally", and do *not* comply with the theory of cause and effect?

But looking more closely at chance events, events that happened apparently without rhyme nor reason, one can see that they recur constantly. Which brings us to the question of probability, and consequently, the theory of probability.

This theory is able to predict, with inexplicable precision, the total result of processes involving a large number of individual events, each one of which on its own is unpredictable. In other words, a large number of uncertain events produce a certain event, a large number of chance events lead to a very definite result. As such, this is a paradox, yet it seems that it happens that way in practice.

According to Schopenhauer[1], the "casual" is a meeting in time of elements unconnected by causality.

«Physical causality is only one of the governors of the world; the other is a metaphysical entity, a sort of universal consciousness, in comparison with which individual consciousness is like a dream compared to the waking state».

Pauli[2] declared that there are non-causal, non physical factors, which operate in nature and which are essentially still not well understood. According to Jung[3], "synchronicity" is the simultaneous happening of two events linked by meaning, but not by causality, or a coincidence in time of two or more events that are not in a causal relationship to each other, but have the same or similar meaning, equal in degree to causality, as an explanatory principle.

Jung theorised that meaningful coincidences, which he termed synchronistic events, indicated a "self-existent meaning" based on an order of the macrocosm and microcosm, independent of our will; and furthermore that synchronicity is a phenomenon linked in the first place to psychic conditions, i.e. processes of the unconscious.

According to Jung, the deepest strata of the latter are those of the collective unconscious, potentially common to all those who are part of the human race.

The *decisive factors* in the collective unconscious are the archetypes that make up its structure: a sort of distilled memory of the human race, not to be represented with the words of a language but by elusive symbols common to all mythologies.

We could say that *synchronicity* is the modern term that explains the archetypal belief based on the fundamental unity of all things, which transcends mechanical causality.

Such a definition is virtually identical to the concept of "serialisation" given by Kammerer[4]: the recurrence in time and space of like or similar things or events, unconnected by any single causal agent. It is present in life, just as it is, in nature and in the cosmos; it is the umbilical cord connecting thought, feeling, science and art to the universe which gave birth to them.

It is universally accepted by physics that coincidences tend to come in series, and that these coincidences are manifestations of a universal principle of nature, which operates independently of physical causality.

According to Kammerer, coincidences are only the visible tips which "by chance" have caught our attention, because our habits tend to have us ignore the ever-present manifestations of serialisation (or synchronicity).

In fact we unfortunately only notice the crests of the waves, looking at them as if they were isolated coincidences, overlooking the immensely larger part: the subsiding of the same waves – just as islands seem separate from each other, while really they are the peaks of mountains emerging from the ocean and are part of the earth on which we ourselves stand. It is significant that most inventions are the fruit of Chance, or Luck, understood as *serendipity* [5].

Had Newton walked under the tree a minute before or a minute after, the apple would not have fallen on his head, perhaps then his attention would not have been caught and he would not have begun to work out the theory of gravity.

Going further back in time, if someone had not planted the seed and the tree had not sprung up in that particular place, that apple tree would not have been able to grow, the apples would not have been able to ripen in such a time and that apple would not have come loose to then hit Newton on the head in that particular moment when a certain state of mind allowed him to think constructively.

Quantum physics has led us to a revolutionary way of thinking about the issue of mind vs body.

Sir James Jeans' observation[6] that: «the universe begins to look more like a great thought than a great machine» was not inspired by mysticism, but rather by one of the fundamental principles of quantum theory, the principle of complementarity. According to this principle, as de Broglie[7] defined it, the known elements of matter behave, in certain circumstances, like incorporeal waves; in others, like solid particles.

The electron is, at one and the same time, a solid body and a wave.

Bohr[8] defined this subatomic duality as the "principle of complementarity".

In the cosmos and the subatomic microcosm, the immaterial aspects dominate; in both, matter dissolves into energy and energy dissolves into an infinity of forms and configurations of something that, at present, defies all physical research. For Wheeler[9] the stage on which the space of the universe moves is certainly not space itself. No-one can be the arena they are in; they must have a vaster area in which to move, and the area must be something greater, endowed with an infinite number of dimensions.

Eddington[10] said that the substance of the world is the substance of the mind. What modern physics calls *complementarity* agrees perfectly with Cartesian dualism of mind and matter.

Atoms are not things said Heisenberg[11]: at the atomic level the objective world ceases to exist both in time and in space, and the mathematical symbols of theoretical physics theory simply refer to a world of possibilities and not facts.

The hard, tangible appearance of things exists only in our world of modest dimensions, the middle range of sizes, measured in pounds and yards which our senses are used to. Both on a cosmic scale and on a subatomic scale this tangible relationship reveals itself to be an illusion.

Reality is relative to the subject, to the individual observing it. There is diversity of points of view, precisely arising from every single person: this is "subjective reality", the only one that is true for every single observer. If reality were objective, we would all be alike, we would think in the same way, we would have the same tastes.

Thus reality is always subjective: and since there is no objective reality, there cannot be a fictional reality.

For example: in a locked, isolated room, half the people present, who have been hypnotized, see a watch on the table, the others do not see it. Which are right? Both are, as they all express subjective reality.

14

Contrary to the conviction of some scientists who maintain that the movement of matter is not influenced by consciousness, although consciousness is obviously influenced by the movement of matter, Wigner[12] observed that matter is likely to be influenced by what it influences.

Furthermore he affirmed that consciousness alters the usual laws of physics, in that there is no known phenomenon where an object is influenced by another, without, in its turn, exerting some influence on the latter.

Capra[13] on the other hand declared that what is called an "isolated particle" in reality is the product of its interaction with what surrounds it, such that it becomes impossible to separate one part of the universe from the rest.

Bohr also rejected any description that considered observation and an observed system as separate.

According to the so-called "Mach principle", the inertia of all earthly objects is determined by the total mass of the universe. This implies that not only does the universe influence local events but also such local events influence the universe.

Whitehead[14] declared that any local agitation shakes the whole universe and the effects at a distance, as imperceptible as they are, do exist. A detached self-contained existence is not possible, everything is united, no atom is an island, the microcosm mirrors the macrocosm, and is mirrored by it.

Lastly, Vedantic philosophy itself affirms that the perceived object cannot be separate from the mind of whoever perceives it; the observer and the observed constitute a single, indivisible, fluid reality: I am you and you are me. These are concepts that are found in the teachings of all the philosophies and esoteric schools of the world. Thus mysticism and official science are finally converging.

And, as John Weightman[15] wrote: "I understand that, in reality, I don't understand what I have the illusion of understanding, because language is simply a mirage of comprehensibility in a sea of ignorance".

Fenice Felce (Giampiero Vassallo)

(1) Arthur Schopenhauer (Danzig, 22 February 1788 – Frankfurt am Main, 21 September 1860) was a German philosopher and aphorist, one of the greatest thinkers of the 19th century, and of modern western thought.

(2) Wolfgang Ernst Pauli (Vienna, 25 April 1900 – Zurich, 15 December 1958) was an Austrian physicist. He was among the founding fathers of quantum mechanics. He devised the exclusion principle, for which he won the Nobel Prize in 1945, according to which no two electrons in an atom can have identical quantum numbers.

(3) Carl Gustav Jung (Kesswil, 26 July 1875 – Küsnacht, 6 June 1961) was a Swiss psychiatrist and anthropologist.

(4) Paul Kammerer (Vienna 17 August 1880 - Puchberg am Schneeberg 23 September 1926) was a biologist and thinker.

(5) Serendipity is a neologism which etymologically derives from Serendip, ancient name of Ceylon. It means the good fortune of making unexpected discoveries by pure chance, or finding something completely different from what you were looking for.

(6) Sir James Hopwood Jeans (Ormskirk, 11 September 1877 – Dorking, 16 September 1946) was a British astronomer, mathematician and physicist, whose contribution was based above all on the application of mathematics to physics and astronomy.

(7) Louis-Victor Pierre Raymond de Broglie, known for short as Louis de Broglie (Dieppe, 15 August 1892 –Louveciennes, 19 March 1987), was a French physicist and mathematician.

(8) Niels Henrik David Bohr (Copenhagen, 7 October 1885 – Copenhagen, 18 November 1962) was a mathematician, philosopher developing the philosophy of science, theoretical physicist and academic.

(9) John A. Wheeler (Jacksonville, 9 July 1911, Hightstown, NJ 13 April 2008, was an American physicist.

(10) Sir Arthur Stanley Eddington (Kendal, 28 December 1882 – Cambridge, 22 November 1944) was an English astrophysicist.

(11) Werner Karl Heisenberg (Würzburg, 5 December 1901 – Munich 1 February 1976) was a German physicist, winner of the Nobel Prize for physics in 1932, considered one of the founding fathers of Quantum Mechanics.

(12) Eugene Paul Wigner, born Jenó Pál Wigner (17 November 1902, 1 January 1995) Hungarian American physicist, winner of the Nobel Prize for physics in 1963.

(13) Fritjof Capra, (Vienna, 1 February 1939) Austrian systems theorist and essayist, became famous for *The Tao of Physics* in 1975, translated in Italian in 1982 (Adelphi). He also wrote about sustainable development, ecology and theory of complexity.

(14) Alfred North Whitehead (Ramsgate, 1 February 1861 – Cambridge, 30 December 1947) was a British philosopher and mathematician.

(15) John George Weightman, 29 November 1915 – 14 August 2004, was an English writer and newspaper columnist.

THE CONCATENATION
OF EVENTS

The universe is composed of a very dense spider's web of events interacting with each other, yet human beings do not always discern the laws that govern them.

Synchronicity can be defined in many ways: as the interaction between the temporal moment and the event, as the possibility of gathering events from the impossible and making them become not only probable but certain, as will transformed into an action and a precise choice, representing the maximum probability conceded by free will. Synchronicity is present in all space and at all times, like a great sea in which creatures are ever and always immersed.

Synchronicity thus presupposes on the one hand the existence of a web of events that design the universe and on the other the existence of creatures that participate in this great universal design and that perceive, in a more or less conscious fashion, the synchronistic connections.

And all creatures carry within them the elements of synchronicity in that they have to interact with other living forms, owing to their very nature.

Human beings often behave in such a way as to be impervious to the synchronistic Forces. It is for this reason that they lose the possibility of commanding a wider perspective of the reality in which they live.

The synchronistic opportunities are directly connected to time, which allows the creation and destruction of forms.

If we imagine the universe to be woven with lines corresponding to different events, and if we, as living beings, were to find ourselves at a point in the middle of these lines, we could, thanks to our free will and the level of knowledge attained, bend them or, even better, extend ourselves outwards to be able to understand a greater number of event-lines.

18

Synchronistic events can be apprehended through the signs that continually appear to us.

Consider a practical example. Someone travelling by car, sees a bird on their left and at the same time gets a puncture. The following year, they again see a bird flying on their left and instinctively the earlier episode springs to mind.

They stop the car and get out to check the wheels, and discover there is something sharp in the road right in front of the car. They thus discover that a like event brings a similar result even if at a different time; which increases the possibility of prediction: thus all events that seem to be chance may be considered synchronistic.

Synchronicity is expressed through the use of our power to act on forms and on time itself, on events that may be far apart (a concept that has been defined as the "power of Maya").

The laws of synchronicity are constant because they are based on the maximum uncertainty principle.

In one unit of time an infinity of possible events could occur: being hit by a meteorite, falling off a chair that breaks, finding a ten-euro note on the ground, getting up, sitting down, sneezing and so forth.

It is a case of events that come into the field of possibilities but with a very low probability of happening in any single unit of time.

If one could dilate this unit of time and transform a second into a million years, in such a long period of time it could be that one came across millions of such ten euro notes at certain points of space and time or find a chair that breaks endless times.

Synchronicity is that Force which allows us to go beyond the probabilities linked to time, dilating the possibility to infinity, so as to succeed in reeling in even the most improbable of events, making it condense – manifest – in one's own time.

Drawing on the religious experiences of ancient peoples, this Force can be called "chance", since in the Greek pantheon there existed two entities who were above all gods: Chance and Chaos.

Chaos is the undetermined, the whole mixed up, the collection of elements without order, beyond any organisation whatsoever.

19

Chance on the other hand, is that great ordering entity which is above the different divinities and which rules the destiny of gods and men.

The energy of creative thought is the element that enables synchronicity to increase; in fact the greater the knowledge, the more numerous are the synchronic events that can happen.

By applying the theory of synchronicity we can identify a series of elements that permit the interpretation of different phenomena (events commonly termed *paranormal*) according to a broader perspective, leading to a better understanding of them.

For example, it is precisely the fundamental laws of synchronicity that provide us with an explanation for telekinetic phenomena

According to the theory of unstable equilibrium, human thought acts more easily on a precariously balanced object because it is easier for us to think that an object on the edge of the table might fall than one placed in the middle of the table.

Experiments of this kind have shown that objects thought of clearly and precisely will fall in a shorter than average time, according to calculations of probability. Thus one can theorise that by means of our own aura (energy field) we may operate on the lines that travel through space, acting on the atoms themselves that make up objects. In this way one succeeds in bringing a probable, or possible, event from the future time into manifestation in the present.

For example: by placing a vase in an unstable position, and then going one, ten, twenty years into the future, or perhaps ten centuries into the future, the possible event of the vase falling for some reason will be located.

Thus a possibility is collected from the future, since in a sufficiently ample period many possible events will be realised, so that one can choose a particular one that is of interest, to bring it into the present.

Even the healing brought about through pranotherapy finds its explanation in the laws of synchronicity. The pranotherapist acts as a catalyst for synchronicity, and represents the element through which one operates by "fishing" across time for the condition of health; this effect also manifests when for example a person begins to feel better as soon as they have made a doctor's appointment: it is not a case of a simple chance event but a broad action of the interaction of events according to synchronicity.

On the Earth, synchronicity condenses to a greater or lesser degree according to the rate of flow of the Synchronic Lines, which, as we shall see below, constitute a kind of spider's web of Forces that envelopes the whole planet.

Condor Girasole (Eugenio Mensi)

21

THE SYNCHRONIC LINES

The energy streams of planet Earth

WHAT ARE
THE SYNCHRONIC LINES

P roviding a single definition of the Synchronic Lines turns out to be an arduous proposition. We could say that in the first place they are torrents of energy capable of catalysing the great Forces present in the Cosmos.

Every world is born out of chaos: through the Synchronic Lines and their distribution of intelligent orders, chaos transforms into chance – that is, the synchronic condition is formed which allows for the creation of a very large quantity of events.

25

The Synchronic Lines are the roads of life, which join all planets where life exists: they collect and distribute life. All living beings travel these streams, like paths in the forest, like the torrents that carry water and life everywhere. Thus they can flow more easily in an oasis than into the desert. They are streams that flow at a constant pace, carrying much subtler substances than air or water, a kind of energy not easily measured which represents not only life but also information that needs to travel through all planets.

One component of the Synchronic Lines is the non-substance substance [NSS][1].

When a movement of the Lines, which has its own vibration, meets the complexity of a functioning system - in this case an ecological life system going from the physical to the spiritual – then NSS can be formed.

It is not something that can appear anywhere, when it happens it surfaces on the form of small islands, so we can collect it.

The non-substance substance can be rendered dense in a practical way thanks to the use of the large *selfs* made of copper – while not stable, it represents an ideal line of connection with the Synchronic Lines, acting as a sort of conductor or detector.

Thanks to intention, and suitable precise systems and rituals, the form is defined and will then appear on the Lines, since it positions in a sort of middle frequency, and is absorbed and distributed by the Lines. The images projected by human beings on the Lines are first translated into this non-substance substance.

By utilising the non-substance substance it is possible to form different types of lens that can refract the signal and influence a very broad area, modifying the flow of events. The Force that moves in this energy stream reacts where it meets life and can also be transmitted with spirals, the system that was used before control of the Lines had been achieved.

There is however a noticeable difference between an energy which is in itself amorphous and can be modified by thought, and another kind of energy which takes on stability in continual movement and which above all cannot be modified by thought: this is the energy peculiar to living planets.

The Synchronic Lines are decidedly not magnetic earth lines nor are they influenced in their movements by planets and nearby stars, rather the opposite, the influence on this network increases in proportion to distance in space.

The Lines are influenced instead by the apparent position of the stars seen from the Earth. For example, the stars which make up the constellation of the Great Bear have no relationship among themselves from the point of view of astrophysics, yet nevertheless the apparent planetary positions seem to have an influence from a terrestrial point of view upon the distribution of Syncronic Lines on the planet.

27

The Synchronic Lines may flow above or below the earth's surface; when they are close to ground level, it can be easier for us to contact them, thanks to the construction of secondary Lines, the Minor Lines, constructed with Forces connected to human thought.

The Minor Lines influence human beings, with ramifications that can carry instructions, information, amplification from the Major Lines.

It has taken many years to draw the map of the Lines and it will take yet more to improve it and make it more extensive: the work being done also includes physical journeys throughout the world, researching and retracing plans of variation in possible events; this way several series of repeating patterns of the Lines have been discovered.

By joining together on the map similar figures recurring successively over a distance, it can be seen that there are repeating geometric forms found in some areas rather than in others.

It was then discovered that the Lines are so ancient that they determined the formation of mountains and the course of rivers.

It was realised that a huge quantity of thought energy is needed to utilise them. The people of antiquity built sanctuaries or temples in the places where they surfaced, places where prophetic dreams or healing happened more easily.

Thus they set out to manage these Forces, raising for example menhirs as antennae to tune into points higher off the ground.

28

[1] Non substance-substance (NSS) is a form of subtle energy that can be shaped by thought, which is to be found at a height from the ground of between 50 and 130 cm.(20 inches and 5 ft.). Its main characteristics are its volatility and freshness, since it is free of express time fractions and, therefore, can be used for many purposes. It is comparable to a blank page, on which you can write independently by events. It becomes denser particularly in the areas crossed by the Synchronic Lines, and so rich in life and complexity. It is used for specific alchemical operations.

THE FUNCTIONS AND USE OF
THE SYNCHRONIC LINES

In the present historical period Italy finds itself in a particularly favoured position having many points of contact with the Synchronic Lines. Val Chiusella, north of Turin, was chosen as the site for Damanhur precisely because it is where four major Lines meet.

The Lines make it possible to propagate ideas in an extraordinary way. Information can be fed into or received from them. If someone goes for a walk, for instance, in a place where one of them passes, the thoughts emitted by that person may be gathered up and transmitted throughout the planet.

At times these points are the places from whence fashions originate, innovative ideas arise, and so on. In fact there exist places and conditions which seed great waves of thought: if someone were to sleep on a Synchronic Knot which has a correspondence with the whole planet - that is, a crossing point or passing point of Minor Lines - and were to dream all night of (say) ice-cream, within a few days there could be a wave on the planet of wanting ice-cream.

These points of diffusion are called "sources of the Nile". A colour can come into fashion in this way: whoever has the rare knowledge of how to use the Lines, can

29

condition a huge number of individuals on the Planet through them.

By now almost all of these Lines are known; one also knows their inner map, which is a million times more complex than the outer one.

At the points where they surface, the Lines can be perceived even without being a sensitive: the environment may seem quite different and time may have a different value because there may be transformations from a psychic point of view. However they are particularly perceptible to people trained according to precise codes and protocols, the case for example of the specialist researchers known as "dreamers".

30

The ancient Chinese coined the term "Dragon's Back" referring to the Synchronic Lines, having noted their continual undulating movement with respect to the surface of the Earth, similar to the scales on the back of a dragon. They are called Dragon's Back Lines, too, because they have a very irregular course: owing to the influence of rivers and mountains, they may take on very contorted or convoluted forms.

The Synchronic Lines shift with the passing of the millennia, very slowly, following precise rules creating a very real network. In antiquity an important temple could arise only on some particular crossing of Lines of this kind, and in that way the priests were able to manipulate the Forces linked to the various divinities and earth entities.

On the points where these lines surface, if one knows how to do so, energies very important for the evolution of humankind can be contacted, but today the knowledge enabling this type of contact has been all but lost.

There are very important times of the year during which it is easier to contact and utilise the Synchronic Lines: namely the Summer and Winter Solstices. At such times it is as if the Lines become softer, more malleable, making access easier, while in other moments they are more rigid, harder and nothing can so to speak scratch them.

At the times of the solstice the Forces are reduced and better able to be controlled, making it possible to tie in other Lines with greater facility, to control or "clean" Minor Lines, to enter into contact with divine Forces at a moment when it is easier to communicate. It is as if there were less "background noise". During the winter solstice the bases are laid for what will eventually be amplified during the summer one.

To render these channels active it is essential to establish points of contact, just as to turn a light on the circuit needs to be closed. These currents can precipitate far-reaching events. Summing up, these lines have a variety of important functions:

1) they are able to influence or change events;
2) they are the highways used during high-level astral travel;
3) they can carry ideas, thoughts and moods and influence all living creatures;
4) they represent the principal nervous system of our planet, understood as a being in its own right;

5) they are highways of communication from and to the rest of the Universe.

The Synchronic Lines are the special means of communication which become amplifiers of emotion; information is transmitted on the Lines in a way that it can arrive through dreams, by means of images, using an emotional and not necessarily linguistic language.

For this reason such signals can be received independently of any language or culture.

Every living creature has the possibility of contacting the synchronic Forces.

As was known many, many centuries ago, human beings in particular could travel throughout the universe, at more or less infinite speed. In fact other creatures also know to make use of these synchronic Forces: trees for example receive and send information linking up with the entire universe by means of the Lines. At present, the plant world is perhaps the one that at certain levels makes best use of the synchronic Forces.

When by chance you stumble on a point of access to the Lines, you will be able to receive but not send, it is like being in front of a monitor screen: you can receive the picture but you do not have the camera to transmit.

When one enters a Synchronic Line there is always the risk of not being able to finding the way back, since by their nature the Lines never surface in the same point they departed from but move along the course of their lines of flow: close to the poles the Lines converge, they wind around each other and then move off towards other worlds. In these places it is easier for there to be gateways that open in all directions: in these cases doorways allowing the passage from one Line to another continually open and close.

Among the various possibilities open to those who know these Forces, it is even possible to programme one's own incarnations: whoever knows how to enter into contact with the Synchronic Lines can choose the place and time of their rebirth. In the After Life, all souls travel along the Synchronic Lines because they are the only road which will take them in a given direction.

In fact the soul follows the direction of the physical body using the roads of life – the Synchronic Lines. If you want to know which are the inhabited worlds, all that is needed is to follow the Lines where they will lead. These planetary roads become denser as more life travels them, in the same way as a path: the more it is trodden, the more visible it becomes, until it is a road.

33

Among these inhabited planets there exists a very real transmigration of intelligent life, of souls, which at times is blocked or limited for complex reasons. In this way one can incarnate on many other worlds, coming from or going on afterwards to worlds different from our own. The experience of this type involves planets that are being tested, and this is how the Earth might be considered from certain points of view.

It is known that some time ago the Earth received a kind of seal, a quarantine, preventing the exit of souls, so it became essential to remove this block to rebalance the situation and allow a circulation of souls in both directions. Humanity will now be newly enriched by the influx of experiences, becoming involved in the evolutionary situations of other worlds.

The various "race minds"[1] have to meet in the Synchronic Lines for a series of reasons: the flow of experiences is to be found in any case in this labyrinth since such streams contain bursts of energies, experiences, memories linked to the form which has maintained and lived them.

The race mind itself is not contained in anything, but form must be in some way memorised as an element and so it must be contained in an energy stream. The only point of contact with the other aspects of existence, between the material world and the like time flow, is thanks to a reality which passes through all these expressions, the reality of the Lines.

Notice that the Synchronic Lines can become polluted: it depends on the way in which they are used.

Within the Lines there is a current of synchronicity which, as a law is not uniform in its distribution upon form: it enters into the maintenance of every form but has also the ability to manifest outside every individual form, or act on it giving it a different weight, somewhat as if it were gravity, to every form.

Thus, every form influenced in this way to exist necessarily has a quantity of synchronicity established with that particular basic equilibrium, but it may have a differ-

34

ent weight: this synchronicity can give different weights to the objects, thus an object may be more or less synchronic and thus may weigh a gramme or a kilo.

This aspect may vary, depending on the strength of the current in the Lines; we are looking at a Force which can manifest by interacting with other forms, with a particular form. At times this form will be complex, a living form for instance, but this is not always so. All this as a whole produces complexity, but not confusion.

Beyond the essence of the object - from the macroscopic and microscopic point of view – that object has the possibility of exerting influences on other objects that are different from those that it would naturally exert. In short, this is a formidable variable.

35

[1] Race minds are the containers that conserve and process the experiences of every living species.

THE USE OF THE
SYNCHRONIC LINES IN TIME

The Synchronic Lines are able to conserve an infinite quantity of knowledge, as if they were the bibliography of everything that has been thought and organised at the level of thought.

It is thus possible to draw on the information, on images and visions of various events that have taken place in the past - one can also foresee with a certain accuracy where events linked together will happen, even if they are difficult to see singly with other systems since they leave no definite traces. Foreseeing what will happen in the future, it becomes possible to modify the present.

It is evident, therefore, that whoever succeeds in making use of these Forces may act on a very large number of probable events, which will more easily transform into real ones.

By having control one can act on the Synchronic Lines so as to generate within them a series of little pressures consisting of 600 thousand million actions per second so as to obtain the desired changes on the leading edge of the time wave.[1]

Throughout the millennia, these Lines have been used in particular to change events: in some cases, they have etched deeply upon history.

37

The Synchronic Lines were known at the time of Christ and in part were used, but their use waned in importance because social contacts of the time were limited to the immediately surrounding areas, so it was pointless spreading thought throughout the whole planet.

The Lines were considered preferential energy channels leading from one point to another. In those days they used instruments of another kind, with a range of use limited to narrow social territories.

The Synchronic Lines can take on numerous functions: whoever knows their entrance points is able to produce changes in the way of thinking of the planet, to utilise magical Forces better, to contact quasi divine energies, entities of very great power. To utilise the Synchronic Lines means having new energies at one's disposal for the planet.

In contact with the power of the Synchronic Lines it is possible to spread a thought to any corner of the globe, but to do it requires a complexity of know-how possible only for those who have very high levels of knowledge, in the purest sense of what is called Magic: whoever is capable of using the Lines can travel across and beyond our universe, as well as communicate with other species.

The Lines pass over the Threshold, the world intermediate between the world of Form and the Real[2], carrying the potential for complexity from one place to another. Their function is thus that of allowing non-material aspects of complexity to travel, to move across the worlds.

38

Those who had suitable knowledge went along these channels by astral travel and other similar techniques, in order to project themselves to any point on the planet. Whoever has learned in astral projection to move a fair distance from their bodies may have come across these great shining Lines, which normally, however, one cannot approach, since they repel you just as one positive magnetic pole does to another.

Appropriate knowledge is needed to enter them: the work that is carried out through the Lines has been established for centuries and millennia. It is not merely enough to send a message on the Lines and assume it will get there: to send a message does not necessarily mean that someone will read it.

Receiving represents a very complex part of the message; it may not happen for example because a contrary Force prevents the communication, acting in opposition to modify or reduce the message. Then it also depends on the spiritual level of the receiver: these may be human or animal.

The action of the message may concern events that are due to happen, in which case one has to know how to apply a series of happenings relating to the event, to be able to alter the reading of the message.

According to tradition, very ancient and evolved peoples, such as the Etruscans or the great Central American civilisations, could have deliberately disappeared off-planet, to contact other parallel universes, precisely thanks to their ability to make use of these synchronic Forces.

39

In fact it is said that by knowing how to manage these channels it might be possible to pass into parallel worlds, that is, worlds that vibrate at a slightly different rate to ours.

When we did not yet have access points to the Lines, spirals were used to enter them, at great cost due to the very large quantity of energy required to "puncture" a Line as if it were a mosquito sting piercing a blood vessel.

These particular spirals had a cost at times higher than the benefit that could be got from them. But the function in that case was not to get energy but rather to open up spaces in order to be able to enter and modify or exclude passages of Minor Lines.

40

It is like a war which has its cost and its calculation includes expenditure of a huge amount of energy to gain what at the time seemed a scant gain, knowing that later on this little could prove to be the straw that tips the balance.

If one controls a Line, then the energy needed can be taken from it, but this cannot happen if there is not control of the Line: at the start of the work of freeing the Lines we did not have this option. There are very few "synchronic doorways", although they do exist: at the beginning there were a few small points of this sort on the Lines.

The problem was that the greater part of the Synchronic Lines was controlled by other Forces. However, being able to enter at various points with the right strategy with the energy we had previously obtained, we could set out to do what we ultimately succeeded in doing.

[1] The farthest front of the time wave (or leading edge of the wave) is the maximum most advanced moment of time from which the so-called "test time" started to be build in order to replace the old time line along which humanity would otherwise come to an end.

[2] Threshold, Form and the Real: as Form is the field of laws regulating the physical universe where we find ourselves while we are alive, the Threshold is the state of being which no longer has need of the relationship with Form to be maintained. Instead, it gathers in the results of complexities obtained in Form (life experiences, memories, information...) and all the complexity issuing out of Form but yet still too incomplete to attain the Real. The Real is the highest concept of Being, Truth. The souls in formation, in their journeys entering and leaving physical bodies pass through the Threshold, by using the Synchronic Lines.

THE NERVOUS SYSTEM
OF THE UNIVERSE

The various planets are linked together through their central suns. There exists a sort of great network superimposed on our galaxy which enables the solar systems to be linked together: the Lines can thus be seen as a sort of nervous system of the creature we call the universe.

The reference point here is the central sun of each system, as if it were the meridian of reference: a solar system with various planets. Conventionally it is said that the Lines of the planets go in the direction of their sun. We could draw a map of the network of Lines that link the various points of the galaxy. There are Lines that unite the manifestations of life among the planets, between one solar system and another.

Comparing it to our brain one could say that the various inhabited planets correspond to synapses and neurons. From the universal Lines that join planets and solar systems, the regional Lines spread out into the life centres, our planet included.

At the point where a universal Line touches the sun, for example, it divides into smaller Lines which carry power, energy and information to the sun itself. The lines are the network that keeps the planet united.

43

Thus in future it might be possible to discover other forms of life in the galaxy by following the path of the Synchronic Lines. At the points of major presence of life, the Lines form loops of a sort: thanks to these formations we can identify the planets that host life.

To know where there may be planets inhabited by evolved life forms all we need to do is to observe the size of the Synchronic Lines inside the galaxy. It is like saying that a busy highway probably leads to a city, whereas a footpath would lead more likely to a hut.

The Synchronic Lines come out of the poles of the planet where they join together, to then go on their way: they are the roads that life travels down to carry the diffusion of knowledge-awareness from one form to another, from one point of the universe to another.

The galaxies are in their turn joined by even greater highways and have a tendency to shift and reunite where synchronic knots are formed. All this suggests the existence of stellar empires.

The shifting of the galaxies in the universe tends towards those places where Lines, which sometimes take on strange characteristics, can become dense. For example, in some places they tie together and form doorways into other universes.

Thus crossing points are created, with which one can get into contact with universes on different vibrational planes.

Notice also, that despite the movement of the planets, there is a constant, continuing relationship between the universal lines and the planets themselves.

When an interplanetary line touches a planet, the line divides into a large number of channels, which form a grid. The Lines that meet a planet get deflected and arrive at a right-angle.

If in the economy of the universe these Lines were to slow down in relation to the speed of rotation of the planet and were to detach completely, life on the planet would cease. The law of chance (synchronicity) would not work and cells would be formed without respect for the harmony of life.

Synchronicity is the Force of the universe which allows laws to be given to all the other Forces – electromagnetism and gravity for example. And the particles which rotate around an atom do not collide because they respond in a perfect manner to this law.

By utilising the Synchronic Lines to travel one does not make a linear journey, but in reality one moves on them by bending space.

The Red Lines, the ones that run north-south, are projected into space moving in two opposite spirals that widen out into the rest of the universe. These spirals join the Earth to all the other bodies existing in space.

Through the Synchronic Lines it will be possible to calculate and measure space travel, if only because no other type of energy allows us to obtain information as easily.

When mankind begins to venture into the universe, we shall be able to use the Synchronic Lines to pinpoint the position of our own planet and the point we want to reach.

45

The Synchronic Lines are the means of communication most used by the various inhabited systems inside the galaxy. So not radio or electromagnetic waves but rather the rational use of the energies carried by the Lines.

The Lines are therefore a kind of preferential channel capable of linking different, extremely distant worlds with different time and gravitational conditions, differences which in this case are utterly irrelevant because life flows according to its own rules. The Synchronic Lines enable the creation of a kind of space fabric suitable for sustaining such a wave front.[1]

For example around the solstices, our planet emits a particular signal that contains information gathered from the plant world, a signal which travels through the universe and reaches other worlds in such a way as to spread uniformity or benefit from the experimentation already done elsewhere. Basically we are looking at the universe economising.

On Earth, human beings of our type being symbiotic creatures, make use of the trees. The trees live in symbiosis with us and can represent the bridge across which signals are emitted inside the galaxy, to give precise information on the human race and on other species. During the solstices trees have an explosive amount of life energy.

For this reason it is easier to utilise the Lines in such periods. The different forms of life tend to influence one another, which is why, in the long term, there is a relative stability within the universe.

It is important to remember that whatever comes into contact with the Lines undergoes precise changes: looking at the data systematically ones comes across, for example, differences of temperature and humidity. The vegetable world as an element of amplification can manage to create networks of this kind quite easily, thus it can be made use of for direct experimentation.

47

---

(1) The leading edge of the time wave (or wave front) is the most advanced edge of time from where one sets out to construct the so-called "trial time", to replace the time line in which humankind would have otherwise met its end.

THE DISCOVERY OF THE SYNCHRONIC LINES

The beginning of the science fiction story we are telling, lies some 75,000 years in the past. The Lines were formed at a moment in time owing to their being inhabitable within the concept of the developing complexity of life.

Their discovery on the Earth at first marked a very important event, as it happened while exploring the significance of death. By observing the path of the dead, it was noticed that all the deceased went in the same direction. It was then understood that there must be something special here.

49

There are species that make use of forms of sensitivity and by their nature they can see the Lines and the points of power: it is a matter of exploring with the senses, understood culturally in a different and broader way than we are used to. To begin with it was thought that there was a specific point relating to death, presided over by the divine Forces connected with that particular territory and civilisation, then it was discovered that there were subdivisions of the subtle bodies that did not stay there where they were meant to.

Later on, drawing on the ability to recognise and follow the past lives of the various forms, it was noticed

that the personalities and basic characteristics of individuals in some worlds were to be found on other worlds
too. There had to be a connecting point.

By searching, the traces left by signs of life were found,
revealing the relationship between these life channels
with the various inhabited worlds.

Then it was understood that the roads of life could be
travelled by other signals too: it was realised that there
was an opening to the cosmos at different moments of
the planetary year on different worlds, at times of maximum and minimum vitality depending on the hemisphere
(at least for the worlds where seasons exist).

All this knowledge has been integrated among the
wise and sensitive of various worlds, and they have
worked in close contact with each other to work out the
stellar map of the roads of life.

It was in this context that the discovery arose that stellar maps have continued to exist even after the various
interstellar gateways (also called "portals" or "bridges")
closed, because those maps were linked to the concepts
of directed complexity of which life is a part.

These roads of life, travelled as they are by attractors
and microattractors[1], i.e. by souls, have been identified
for control by whoever had sufficient knowledge. In fact
it was a matter of working with simple paths or indeed
often tortuous and complex ones, since they are subject to the influence of the masses of the suns in the
universe.

50

It was even thought to create further gateways that would remain indestructible, if entrusted to divine Forces vaster than the territorial divinities. Then they mixed religious, philosophical and scientific concepts, succeeding in working out the pathways, the possible rhythms, the alternating of the arrival of souls in the various worlds, the flows of the attractors.

History can also be viewed with this new key to interpretation, taking in a wider panorama: armies might have fought each other not only for commercial or religious reasons or reasons of power as understood in the normal sense, but for control of the Lines.

When, for a series of reasons, there has been need for a "magical war" of several centuries duration, the tendency would emerge to try and occupy the places that allowed access to the sources of power; the requirement was not only to take, occupy, and control the synchronic channels and Minor Lines in order to be able to control more extensive Lines, but also to have the possibility of physically occupying places where perhaps Lines did not pass but were nevertheless important because they held symbols and keys to the Forces.

Every world emits a unique signal. Since the Earth had been excluded for a long time from the transference of souls, there was a consequent expansion of its Lines; these Lines, from the moment they are formed, remain stable: rather it is the continents that move.

Once the Lines which otherwise would have been Minor ones were fixed and formed, these in fact became proper Lines in the full sense – that is, they experienced growth as if the internal pressure had increased, but as there was no exchange with the outside, they experienced significant mutation compared with the normal pattern across worlds.

In fact if on average on other worlds there are from five to eight Lines, on our planet there are considerably more: nine horizontal and nine vertical, a total of eighteen general or major Lines.

Hence in the beginning the Lines were not constructed, but came into existence as a result of the blocking of the exits, which is why new internal structures were created; these probably have some passageway not yet discovered.

Not everything about the Lines is known: there are parts and functions as yet unexplored. We have still to explore some of the different levels and conditions of this complex structure. Theories abound but none of them is able to explain all the phenomena of this subject.

---

[1] Attractors and microattractors: The attractor is the intelligent Force that brings the parts making up every individual soul structure together and condenses them. A microattractor puts together specific information and functions.

CONTROL OF THE LINES

I n the universe it is much easier to trade in information and news than in physical objects because
where there is life on the various different planes
it will be easy to reproduce whatever is needed. Even a
free body in space is conditioned and touched by these
Lines which can be imagined as a great fishing net made
of little cubes – three-dimensional squares – of different
sizes, which condition the different forms.

On every planet there exist defensive points which
act as "decompression chambers", to ensure that the
various different living forms can evolve with relative
harmony and with the right differences relative to one
another.

Humanity should have the control and defence of its
own Synchronic Lines: in fact through them both true
and false information can be transmitted, it is for this
reason that the most intelligent life forms try to control every external influence as much as possible, in
self-defence.

The Earth, which we define overall as sentient and intelligent, has its own screens or filters. For this reason
the grid of Lines is a system of layers that wrap around
the planet and form a bottle-neck at both poles, so that
everything passing in or out has to pass the filter.

53

Control over the Lines happens through knowledge of the sequences translated into rhythms, words, sounds and codes which permit access to the various gateways: it is a case in a very real sense of "sound locks".

Numbers can represent the codes of interpretation, of access to the Lines; the very complex sequence for entry and exit from the Lines is based on three principal elements: names, numbers and rhythms.

The Lines open and close on the basis of a very complicated sequence, generally composed of at least thirty elements: by possessing or reconstructing this code one can gain access to the Synchronic Lines. Every Line obviously has its own specific combination even though it is possible to access parts of the Line by knowing parts of the numbers.

In order to contact the Divinity one can use the voice, whistling, other sounds. There are structures composed of music, of sounds, and to enter them one gains access only by sound codes.

For example, as we have said, to enter the Lines there are sound codes and purposely reproduced sounds are used to open and close the gates or crossing points. Even in the operations with the Spheres[1] sound keys can be used. All the sounds that human beings can reproduce are utilised. There are places on the Earth where prime pure sound exists and this happens where there are the shining knots of the Synchronic Lines.

On the Synchronic Lines human beings have discovered frequencies which also relate to the specific use of sound.

In nature we know of internal sounds like the heartbeat, which accompanies us throughout the whole of our lives.

On this planet, because of the specific atmospheric pressure, sound is broadcast according to typical canons. When energy transmissions are made, utilising spheres and Synchronic Lines, the operators know that by projecting "images" of sounds, in reality they are using a signal to transmit something that others also already understand in the depths of their psyche, since what we have to do with here are ancestral sounds.

In order properly to use the sounds, therefore, one must make use of environments that will allow the mind to use the repercussion between material sound and psychic sound to the maximum. Psychic sound has the property of not having material limits, while material sound by its very nature is limited by one's range of perception.

Ritual music employed for energy transmissions of power use a huge range of sounds compared to the perceptive abilities of the senses. This means one hears not only with the ears but also with the whole body, just as colours can be looked upon as the music of the eyes.

The access codes to enter a Synchronic Line are similar to those of a computer; they must be used appropriately and bring with them great responsibility: if mistakes are made, the "Sphere in use" is disactivated and to charge it up and prepare it again will take a lot of time. For this reason it cannot be said that the structure can be kept permanently functioning.

55

At present, vanishingly few individuals are able to control the Synchronic Lines and they are working to bring back balance to a jeopardised system, since the Lines were formerly occupied in good part by a Force inimical to humanity: the phase of liberation and redemption was started precisely thanks to this type of work[2].

There are creatures who control the Lines by controlling the points of access to the Minor Lines. The attempt to take a Minor Line already occupied by others is very difficult.

The difference between a Force that attacks and one that defends itself inside the Lines is huge: if the defender of the line has a potential of one, the attacker must have a potential equal to a thousand.

The type of energy varies in relation to the quantity and length of the Lines under control. The greater the extension of the network of (at least partially) controlled Synchronic Lines, the greater the range of what one can obtain so as to succeed a little at a time in creating proportionately wider networks.

To have complete contact with the whole system means directly accessing the majority of the Minor Lines and thus reducing external interference, even if this does not yet mean governing everything that circulates directly inside the Lines.

The Lines which connect the worlds are not controlled by one Force or another, they are neutral in their own right and anyone can travel down them. Rather, it is the entrances and exits that may be blocked.

In a few rare cases it is possible to have accesses or points of contact through space spirals. Until a while ago (before controlling the Lines) the technology linked to the use of the spiral, to an extent, replaced the Synchronic Lines.

For us the accesses are a representation of reality: they become the object one accesses. The access to something is in reality the object itself, hence the access corresponds to the Synchronic Line itself.

---

(1) The Spheres utilise the laws of Magic which allow one to act outside space-time.

(2) The operation for liberating the Synchronic Lines on this planet was completed in September 1999.

MORPHOLOGY OF
THE SYNCHRONIC LINES
ON PLANET EARTH

A Synchronic Line has a diameter varying between 200 m (220 yards) and 2.5 km (1.5 miles). The largest diameters in general measure around 900 m (975 yards), but in some cases Lines may flatten out greatly to attain a width of around 2.5 km (1.5 miles).

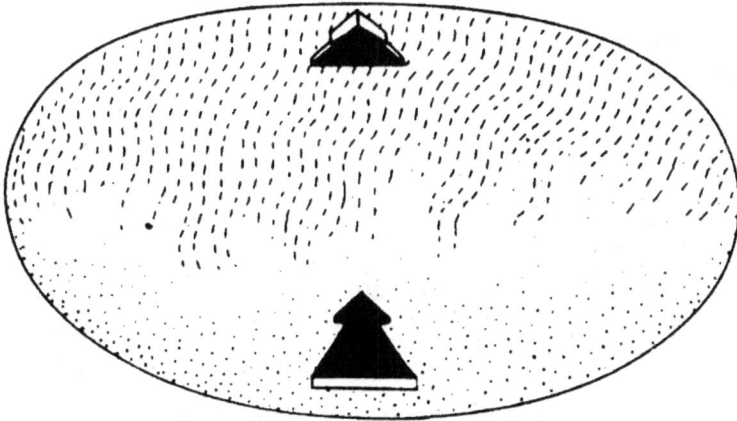

59

Section of a Synchronic Line,
the diameter can measure from 200 m to 2.5 km.

The form taken by these Lines in cross section is a flat-tened oval. Moreover, every Line has two streams flowing in opposite directions, like a highway with one lane in each direction.

Essentially they are two types of energy that balance each other – like a rail line with two tracks for trains going in opposite directions. But in the case of the Lines, the division between opposite directions is not clearly defined.

The Synchronic Lines consist of two streams going in opposite directions and can travel both on the surface and beneath ground and in the sea.

The speed of flow of the energies through the Lines is extremely high, and difficult to quantify with an exact figure.

The energy of the Synchronic Lines of the planet can change density at certain points, where there is more life, and specifically forms of life suited to that density. The density is proportional to what happens inside these Lines: here we have a kind of Moebius ring[1], i.e. a structure capable repeating itself to infinity, which means that as much as it may look like a tube from outside, in reality it is a structure that is apparently like an infinitely widened plane: inside the Line there are no physical dimensions even though there is the plane of flow consisting of two streams or lanes.

Because of mutual influence and the influence of rivers in their courses, as well as the position of the mountains, the Lines take on very contorted forms.

61

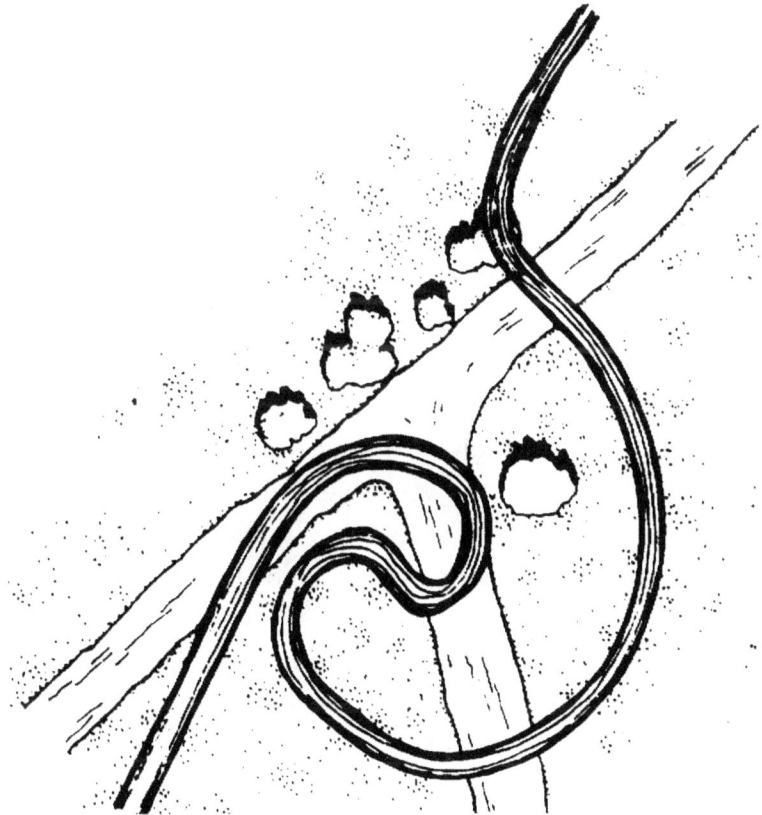

Where they encounter rivers the energy Lines assume spiralling forms.

Given that we are not able to make use of Lines that run too far underground or too high in the air, nor those whose course takes them over the sea, in the sea or under the sea bed, nor those that touch mountains at high altitudes, only about 3-4% of the full extent of the Synchronic Lines around the planet can be accessed for our use.

All these energies are in some way influenced by water: where possible the Lines follow stretches of rivers or are partly diverted – pulled off course – by them.

It is likely that the Synchronic Lines are more attracted by rivers than by anything else: in many cases the Lines flow under the rivers at a depth which varies from a few hundred metres to several miles. The influence generated by the converging of two rivers is particularly powerful: this is the reason why many "magic" cities arose where two rivers meet.

In the seas, on the other hand, the Lines surface where there are islands: compare what happens in physics where electricity is given off by metal points; in other cases, some islands are veritable concentrators of Lines, attracting them like magnets.

Even the clouds can be influenced by the Lines and form odd designs, or they may consistently avoid a certain point in the sky as if running up against an obstacle they had to go around. Underground, at times the Lines are attracted by caverns, including artificially made ones.

For ease we shall use a subdivision into different categories. The General (or Major) Lines, the Minor Lines and the various special Lines.

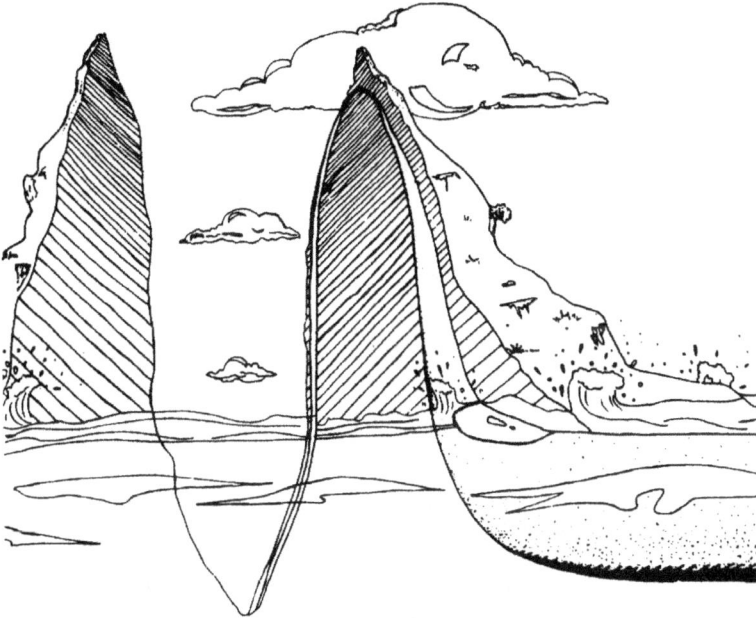

Section showing the mixed current of a Synchronic Line.

The general or major lines are identified by their *apparent* geographical position, in that they may flow on the surface, underground at various depths, in the sea or in the air above the earth's surface.

The general Lines are further subdivided into:

- Nine Vertical or Red Lines (which run predominantly north south and viceversa) and which we identify with the numbers: 1 2 3 4 5 6 7 8 9.
- Nine Horizontal or Blue Lines (which run predominantly east west and viceversa) which we identify with the letters: A B C D E F G H I.

The Vertical Lines draw rather complex shapes over the surface of the planet and have the peculiarity that when they meet at the poles, they form two opposing spirals, which spiral out into space.

These spirals act as antennae for the planet, contact points through which signals arrive from the universe or from whence messages leave, projected by human beings, and other living species – by knowing the appropriate systems.

So to summarize: running pretty well North and South, the nine Red or Vertical Lines converge on each other, bunching together to be projected in a spiralling form into space, while the nine Horizontal (Blue) Lines run their successive journeys around the world. That is, the Horizontal Lines going from east to west and viceversa, form continuous circles and so do not extend out into space.

64

The Lines are actually all linked together, so the division into horizontal and vertical lines is a convention, a working convention to enable us to study them, for as we shall see below, they meet at the centre of the earth. In reality there is only one single stream of synchronicity, which for ease we will identify as Lines at their points of maximum influence: accordingly we can identify such Lines by naming them with letters, numbers and colours referring to the main directions they take going around the world.

We can take it then that, for ease of study, Synchronic Lines fall into two main categories: Horizontal Lines and Vertical Lines.

[1] The Moebius ring, takes its name from its inventor, German mathematician and astronomist August Ferdinand Moebius. (Bad Kösen, 17 November 1790 - Lipsia, 26 September 1868). It is a non-orientable surface, with only one side and only one boundary component.

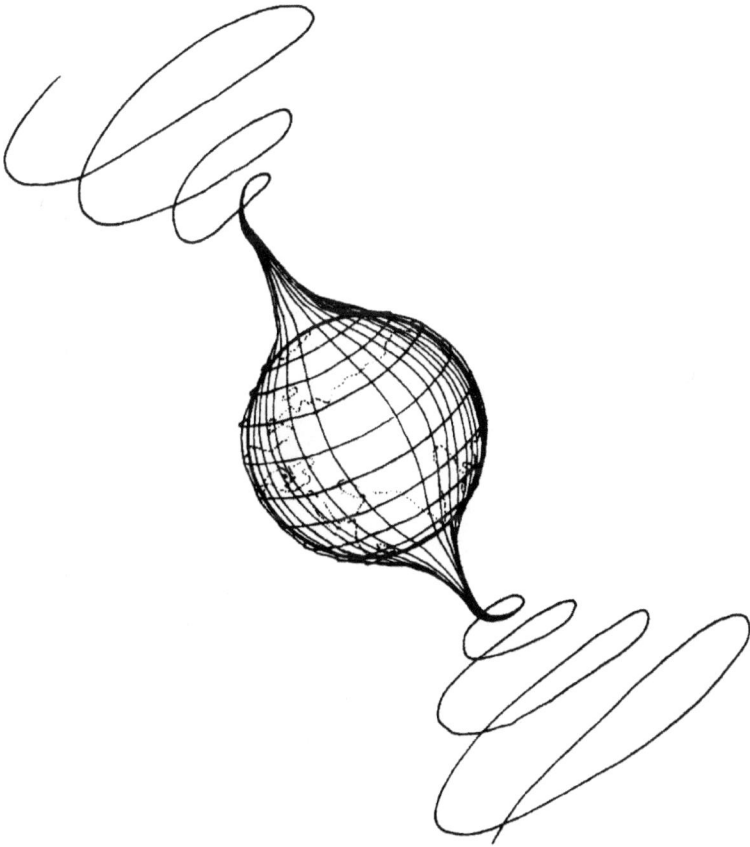

65

At the poles the Vertical lines emerge in a spiral.

THE GENERAL RED
VERTICAL LINES

L et us first take a look at the General (or Major) Vertical Red Lines. To make things simpler we can use the convention of naming the Lines (by numbers, letters and colour) according to the order in which we examine them.

The First Line is the simplest and most linear to follow: for most of its course it runs down the middle of the Pacific Ocean, quite isolated in relation to the others. It puts in a brief appearance on the island of Palmyra an then runs on as far as the South Pole.

67

The Second crosses Canada, goes into the United States following the mountains down the Pacific seaboard, re-enters Mexico, crosses Guatemala and touches a slice of Cuba: it re-crosses Central America as far as Panama, from there it touches a few islands in the Pacific and, keeping about 1,200 miles wide of South America, it at last reaches the South Pole.

The Third is influenced by the Second, which it meets in northern Canada (at their closest point, flowing one below the other, they are only about 22 miles apart): after crossing the United States, passing through Florida the Line reaches Haiti, runs southward to Peru and then, off the coast of South America, it meets the Second a good three times, making a twirling pattern. From there it touches the coast of Chile, moves wide away again, just brushes the tip of Tierra del Fuego before at last reaching the Pole.

The Fourth runs across Greenland, surfaces at a spot in the Cape Verde islands, off the coast of Africa, from where it runs swiftly onward to the south pole.

The Fifth is a very important Line even today. In the past this Line had considerable importance for humanity, when it had greater influence on Egypt, and its energies were catalysed through the Pyramids, a feature which permitted a massive development of magical knowledge among the people of the time.

Historically, it was precisely the engagement of energies utilised through the Minor Fifth and Sixth Lines which allowed the Israelites to gain their freedom and enabled such a close dialogue with their cosmic Divinity (whose name the Israelites did not pronounce): in fact after fleeing from Egypt they wandered for forty years in the Sinai desert following the Minor development of the great Sixth Line, searching for "magical doorways" of access.

The Fifth Line, starting from the north touches the east coast of Greenland, crosses Ireland and southern England – where it is no coincidence that Stonehenge is situated.

It then enters France in northern Brittany and from the summits of the Alps it sweeps down into Italy, several times coming close to the Sixth, touching it, in fact, in a place less than four miles to the north west of Turin.

From there it crosses Tuscany and on down to Rome and into the open sea (here it meets the Sixth again) and passing off the coast of Sicily it touches Crete and immediately afterwards Egypt, brushing the Sixth to make its landfall a few miles from Alexandria, and then running on toward Cairo. From there it crosses Libya and runs down towards Central Africa.

Here it runs close to Lake Victoria and goes on its way forming twirls, down towards the south: at the bottom of South Africa it encounters the Sixth again (as it already did in Italy and Egypt) and here it comes close twice, at a minimum distance of approximately 75 miles. After which it goes on to finish its earthly journey to the South Pole.

The Sixth, starting from the far north, reaches and crosses Finland, enters Russia, Poland, Hungary, brushes Austria and moves into Italy, meeting with the Fifth in two places: the first time less than four miles from Turin and the second time in the open sea more or less level with Rome and half way towards Sardinia.

From here it crosses the Straits of Messina and heads for Greece, crosses Turkey and runs through the Lebanon, Israel and Egypt (where twice over it meets the Fifth) then turns towards the Arabian peninsula, enters the

69

Red Sea, touches the island of Socotra and from there runs down the coast of Africa, crosses Madagascar and enters South Africa where it brushes the Fifth to then cross it again off the coast, in the sea; it then goes on its way to the South Pole.

The Seventh passes over the Urals, crosses the middle of the Caspian Sea, moves west towards Pakistan and Nepal: here on the Everest Plateau it meets with the Eighth five times to then turn sharply south crossing India and in particular following the course of the great rivers.

From here it comes out at the tip of the Indian peninsula and crosses Ceylon. There it surfaces by the south coast of the island in a temple at the centre of Sigiriya.

This Line at last - a unique case among the vertical (north-south) Lines – plunges down toward the centre of the Earth, level with Madagascar, almost in the middle of the Indian Ocean, the only vertical Line not to reach the South Pole.

The Eighth crosses the ex-Soviet Union, follows the mountains and winds around the Seventh along the Himalayas; from here it follows the coast towards Burma and Thailand to touch Sumatra and brush Australia before finally reaching the South Pole.

The Ninth is one of the Lines that flows mostly on the surface. Starting out, it crosses Siberia, most of this on the surface – which makes one think this area might become a land of the future – to then turn, towards China, passing through the mountains. It winds through China before brushing Taiwan and the Philippines, to then double back towards the West (so sharply that at this point it seems to be a horizontal Line). After crossing New Zealand and various islands it reaches the icy wastes of the South Pole.

THE GENERAL BLUE
HORIZONTAL LINES

S o much for the Vertical Lines. Let us now look at the characteristics of the General Blue (horizontal) Lines.

Starting with **Line A**: this line meets the First in Alaska and shortly afterwards meets the Second and Third in Canada: this really rare meeting of three Lines suggests there could be interesting archaeological finds still to come to light in this area.

Line A then crosses into Greenland, just grazes northern Iceland where it meets the Fourth a few miles from the Fifth. It then turns south into Ireland where again it meets the Fifth to then run very close to it in England (this convergence could well be the source of the Celtic civilisation).

Line A then crosses the sea to the Netherlands and runs on down into northern Italy passing through an important knot between the Fifth and Sixth Lines. Then it heads north, brushes the Sixth between Czechoslovakia and Poland, moves into Russia and coasts around the Arctic Circle for a long stretch; from there it meets the Seventh and Eighth, never at a distance of less than 75 miles and joins up with itself in Alaska.

73

Line B draws a wider ring around the planet than Line A: it too passes to the south of Alaska, meets the First off the coast in the Ocean. Then, in the mountains of the United States it touches the Second in three places before brushing the Third on the eastern shore of Lake Ontario, to then plunge into the Atlantic (crossing the Fourth at three points, passing twice above it and once beneath it) making a distinctive twirl in the middle.

74

This twirl or half spiral can be found drawn in more or less identical fashion, by Lines C and D, in the same position in relation to the planetary axis.

There are other several cases of Lines making twirling patterns (half spirals) as they flow: very likely these particular patterns are caused by movements occurring far below the surface and which have thus influenced these Forces in some way.

Line B goes on its way into Portugal, then Spain, France and Italy, where it touches the Fifth and Sixth in five places. In Italy it passes through Emilia Romagna province, almost following the line of the river Po and enters ex-Yugoslavia from the sea. From there it goes into Albania, brushes the north of Greece, crosses Romania and the middle of the Black Sea (where it meets the Seventh).

It then crosses the Caspian Sea, runs on into Russia, and from there into China, where it meets the Ninth in three different places. It then veers towards Korea, running alongside Line C in Japan joining up with itself in the Pacific.

Line C has its source in the Pacific, flowing almost on the surface; in the middle of the ocean it meets with the First, after a long stretch it brushes California, where it crosses the Second three times. It then follows the Californian coast and from there flows on into Mexico, heads south and in Mexico once again meets the Second twice.

It brushes Florida, coming very close to the Third three times (off the north coast of Cuba) it then twirls around in the Atlantic making the same half spiral traced by Line B (meeting the Fourth Line at three points). It then moves into Africa and crosses the Sahara south of Tunisia.

At the Libyan border it moves into the Mediterranean, passing to the south of Sicily. Here it meets the Fifth, brushes the tip of Greece (where it meets the Fifth again) before turning sharply towards the south, running into Egypt where it meets the Fifth and five times the Sixth.

It then follows the Sixth as far as Arabia. It then goes east passing through Pakistan and Iran, meets the Seventh on the Himalayan plateau, brushes Line D and the Seventh, and to the west of Nepal, the Eighth.

Line C then crosses China meeting harmoniously with the Ninth, brushes the tip of Korea, coasts alongside

75

Line B in Japan, touching it in two places and at last in the Pacific it meets up with itself again.

The **Great Line D** surfaces from the depths of the Earth, about 600 miles from Mexico in the Pacific, runs south where it meets the Third off the coast of Peru, then the Second and the Third again (on three levels one above the other) .
It then goes back up towards Panama, moves into South America, winds across Amazonia and follows the course of the River Amazon to reach the Atlantic. Here it too makes that peculiar whirl or half spiral, made also by B and C, and immediately afterwards meets the Fourth, to run onward into the Sahara.

Line D then meets with the Fifth in three places, brushes Libya, follows the Nile in Egypt for a while and continues along the sea coast off Africa and the Arabian peninsula. It then moves back into Africa in the direction of Ethiopia, to then plunge into the Red Sea, where it meets the Sixth in two places.

It then heads north, before once more turning east, running into India. It then touches the Seventh in no less than three places before entering the sea once more; in Burma it almost touches the Eighth at a distance of less than four miles, passes into North Vietnam, almost opposite Hong Kong, meets the Ninth in the Philippines.

Then, after making the same half spiral pattern in the Pacific as it did in the Atlantic, it sinks into the ocean turning downwards towards the centre of the Earth.

Notice that the First Line never meets Line D, nor E or F for that matter.

Line E also surfaces from within the earth in the Pacific, to then disappear once more after completing its journey around the world. It flows mostly along the equator.

This Line first meets the Third and then the Second Line, then reaches Peru, follows the Andes a little, and making that familiar pattern already seen with Lines B, C and D in the Atlantic, heads south crossing Brazil, following a while the great rivers. In the middle of the Atlantic it too meets with the Fourth, to then move into Africa somewhere in the middle (a little above the equator); half way across the continent it goes past the Fifth, carries on and crosses with the Sixth in the Indian Ocean off the coast of Somalia and with the Seventh off the coast between Sri Lanka and the Maldives.

It meets the Seventh twice in Sri Lanka (once almost on the surface, a little above it the second time) from there it goes into Malaysia to meet the Eighth in Borneo, on to New Guinea, and to the east of New Guinea it brushes the Ninth, to then plunge once more into the depths.

Line F is for many reasons an abnormal line. It too has its source under the sea bed in the depths of the Pacific, meeting the Second Line once and the Third twice in a very short space, off the coast of South America. From here it follows the Third a while to the south, crosses it

again twice off the coast of Chile and after all this mean-dering it takes on the South American continent. Here it winds around the mountains and around Earth, surfaces several times, reaches the Atlantic coast and follows it less than 20 miles from the shore.
From the ocean it turns inward following a great river (the River Plate) upstream and then turns back into the sea in the Atlantic where, in the middle, it turns sharply almost at a right angle before passing the Fourth touch-ing it three times.

Next it meanders "hesitantly" around South Africa, crossing the Fifth three times, then goes up through Madagascar winding around the Sixth three times here too. Off the coast of Madagascar, it plunges into the sea and disappears, right where the Seventh similarly sinks into the depths.

But this Line re-emerges 600 miles later and heads for Australia, where it meets the Eighth. Here too it twirls around this continent as it did previously in South America and South Africa, before meeting Line G, touch-ing it twice and receiving energy from it, to finally disap-pear towards the centre of the Earth wide of Australia, without meeting the Ninth.

Line G is a normal horizontal Line in that it joins up with itself, but it has several peculiarities. The most evi-dent one being that it is the most elevated of the great Lines: it flies over the area it passes through at varying heights (for 20% of its journey it runs a few feet above the ground, for 42% of its course it runs at 200 – 275 feet above the ground, and for 33% of the time it runs at heights greater than 900 feet above the ground - as much as 33,000 feet above, in some cases - and just for a small percentage of the time, 5%, it runs underground). It therefore flows predominantly above the Earth's crust and mainly over the sea.

As for its path: it fairly flies over the Pacific, meets the First, the Second, the Third off the coast of South America, then Line F twice, once near the coast then goes through Venezuela and moves off into the Atlantic where it makes the same pattern in reverse as drawn by B, C and D.

Then it glides over the sea towards Africa, barely touching the tip of the continent as if reluctant to be on (or above) dry land, unlike its sister Line F. From here it passes the Fifth and Sixth and heads south as if to avoid the area where Line F and the Seventh sink, and sets down on an island where it brushes Line H for just a small distance as it comes down, to then cross the coast of Australia coming close to the Eighth.

It then meets up again twice with Line F (re-emerging after its disappearance), tracing almost the same shapes as those of the first meeting between these Lines off the coast of South America. It touches the heel of New Zealand and at last joins up with itself once more.

Line H has its own source and it is the only Lines which meets the First Line a good three times in the Pacific.

It then meets the Second and Third still out in the Ocean and just touches the South American coast passing through Tierra del Fuego where it meets Line I. It meets Line I again off the Atlantic coast, from there it too makes that odd half spiral the opposite of those traced in the other hemisphere. It touches the Fourth and then the Fifth and the Sixth far to the south of Africa, it twice meets Line G on an island then it carries on wide of Australia to then meet the Ninth three times to at last end up in its own embrace.

Line I is the shortest of the great Lines since about half of its journey unfurls in an open spiral around the South Pole. It meets the First, the Second, the Third, then meets Line H twice in Tierra del Fuego (this is the only place it touches that has any human population, unlike the other Lines); from here it hints at a pattern in the Atlantic vaguely similar to those traced by the other Lines in that area and immediately afterwards runs onwards overthe South Polar ice.

Although the Lines generally flow where there is more life, Line I for the most part flows through uninhabited areas: this may happen partly because these areas are not inhabited in current times and partly because there may be some kind of life in those regions different to what we are used to thinking of. The Lines are not at the service of humanity but exist independently from it.

Then there are, as in this case, Lines which on looking at the map appear to cross one another, but in reality are farther apart: the minimum distance to be able to say they in effect "brush one another" varies, because it depends on the quantity and speed of the flow of the synchronic functions. For example two Lines further apart but with a very heavy internal flow are closer than two Lines which are geographically closer but which flow at a lower speed. Proximity between the Lines is proportional to the events that can be thus linked together.

In general the three Lines making a complete ring around the world in the southern hemisphere are at least a third weaker than their counterparts in the north, whilst the three middle ones that plunge downward toward the sea-bed are also literally middling as to their energy.

In the present age, which corresponds to the constellation of Aquarius, in particular the Second, Fifth and Sixth Lines are fully "turned on", as are the Horizontal Lines A, B, C. It also seems much power can be catalysed from Lines E and F. The Third on the other hand reduces its own pulsation to the benefit in some way of the Ninth, since what is lost from one is acquired by the other.

In fact it would be possible to draw up a horoscope of the planet by using these Lines as a reference, since they touch many great cities, for as we have seen the civilisations of the past seem to have been built where the influence of these energy streams were felt.

There are cases where it seems that one Line avoids another by plunging downwards or shifting away.

This is an outcome of the way the Lines work: to give an example one can think of the brain synapses or the nerve connections: they are not chance connections but have their right uses. Where there is a major flow or need to connect with other parts, a more intensive branching will occur.

Where instead there is less complexity than in general, this branching will not occur since it would create greater confusion and not greater order (perceiving order out of chaos).This is linked to the greater or lesser utilisation of connections between different elements: so let us take it that this particular nervous system of the planet needs to link together numerous parts.

Areas rich in life may be important connections, yet there are other areas that may be rich in life but where chaos reigns or where life is infinitely disorganised (that is, it is not bound in "ecological" relationship in a spiritually natural sense).

We cannot say that these areas function with or create greater complexity. For example in the past there have been cities that arose well-situated on synchronic connection points.

But then, thanks to different events, and the cities' particular inclinations, they became such negative elements that synchronicity shunned them. The Line might still pass through there, but the actual connection to it will have shifted away.

THE MINOR LINES: WHAT SPECIAL FEATURES DO THEY HAVE

Where these rivers of synchronicity meet, the so-called Minor Lines are evident, and they are a different size to the Major Lines. The Minor Lines are really and truly like exit roads leading off a highway, in that they break away from the "big river": after being separated into two opposite directional flows, the two parts begin to rotate in a spiral around each other, or rather around a central axis. They spiral off to make contact with other general Lines even at great distances.

The average dimensions of the Minor Lines are as follows: the diameter is 3 metres. The maximum distance of rotation of the two subdivisions (or opposite spirals) around a central pivot is about 29 metres.

That is, in non-metric measurement: an average diameter of 9 feet 5 ins, and a spread of 108 feet.

The splitting that gives rise to the Minor Lines almost always occurs as a result of three circumstances:
a) The general Lines are closer together than elsewhere;
b) The Lines are more contorted and tangled;
c) They correspond to particular rivers, islands or mountains.

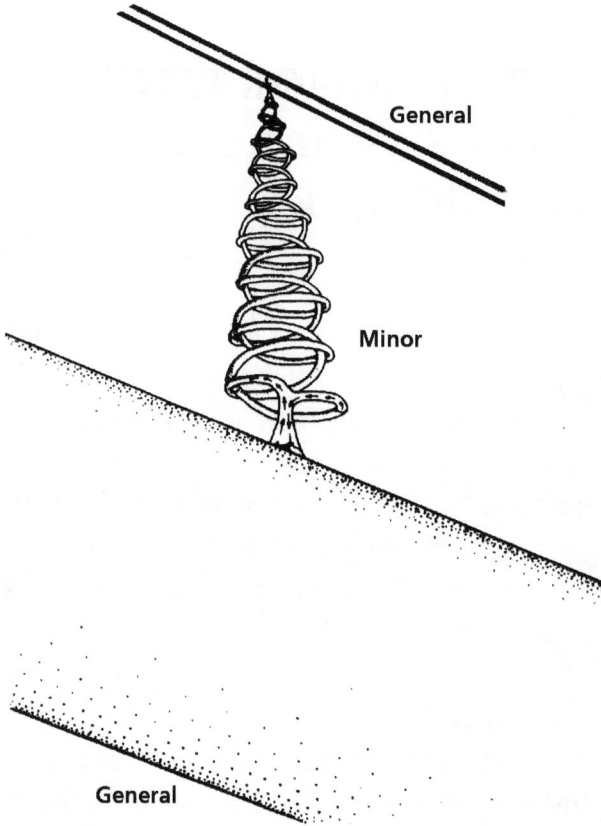

The Minor Lines put the general Lines in contact with each other.

When - in very rare and precious circumstances - the Minor Lines surface, they are doorways that enable us to contact, extract, use and send power from the general Lines. Their flow, which is not generally influenced by any terrestrial Force, is modified by the presence of rivers – or rather, the influence is reciprocal – just as some peaks, or islands arising abruptly from the sea, tend to become antennae for them.

Where rivers meet, the general Lines form bends which allow the Minor Lines to insert themselves more easily: for this reason, as we have said, the magical cities arise where there is a meeting of two rivers.

It is very important to have Minor Lines at one's disposal, which have the function of putting the major Lines in contact at a distance not greater than 12 – 18 miles.

Thus it is possible to input ideas and ways of thinking into the Lines, much like installing programs in a computer: these continue to function as long as there is energy – and since the Synchronic Lines cannot run out of energy, the information remains in the circuit, provided that a suitable "console" does not change the program by inputting new data.

The importance of the Minor Lines lies precisely in the fact that they work like consoles, thus acting like control centres. What is more, the Minor Lines are more malleable, better able to be used: even from a (relatively) physical point of view they can be moulded to take on specific forms.

When a Minor Line joins two major Lines, there will be sufficient energy to obtain two things: firstly energy to keep active the Minor Line so formed, and secondly energy to carry out other operations we can define as "techno-magical".

The Minor Lines allow one to contact – and in certain cases to physically enter – parallel universes, that is worlds overlapping the world we know, which vibrate at a different frequency.

They are in the same place, but the difference in frequency keeps them worlds apart.

There are areas that could be a meeting place for balanced and stable Minor Lines, able to create a natural doorway into parallel universes. There are many places in the world where strange phenomena continually happen, the Bermuda Triangle, is one.

In these cases gravity is altered, with the occurrence of anomalies of various degrees and kinds. However I believe that the Synchronic Lines, by their very nature, are not able to allow the passage of mass. Were they able to do so, in the case of physical phenomena, this would have become known long ago, in the distant past. The discovery that souls can transit from one point to another thanks to the Lines is relatively recent. We are therefore looking at two different things.

Thus it becomes extremely important and worth our while to know where these Forces surface: in general we are looking at places where buried cities or ancient temples can be found and where it is clear that just being near there brings good luck, since it allows important changes to happen: the energy present permits an opening up of individual possibilities in synchronicity.

TO CREATE A MINOR LINE

To form a Minor Line requires a charge of life Forces of huge intensity. There are Lines consisting of the life Force: a living Line characterised by all that is alive and unidirectional, as if there were a pole of reference, for example a particular angle linked to a river or minerals or something similar.

Certain molecules inside everything that grows and is alive in the area, micro-organisms, plants and so forth, are orientated in this specific direction. With the passing of the millennia such particular formations and orientations make an ever deeper mark – compare what happens with molluscs and their precise orientation in alignment with the magnetic poles –. This is like digging out a cave inside a mountain, and finding the resistance of the rock bounded by certain materials.

One can imagine a solid mountain where inside there are points of less resistance compared to what is normal for the mountain itself: so just as water digs out the rock, what is living digs out this passageway, a passage that a little by little joins up these points. The Minor Lines – we could call them caverns of thought – are points which tend synchronically to replicate the great Lines on a smaller scale, the great Lines being the surge of life streaming between the worlds.

87

To put it a certain way: a link to a Minor Line is to the Synchronic Lines what a gold mine is to a large tract of land. The Lines are far more ancient than the mountains. The Earth has been inhabited by living forms for an immense period of time, and by being correctly orientated the living forms have gradually produced these rare links which we call Minor Synchronic Lines.

The Minor Lines, unlike the great Lines, can be damaged by telluric upheavals. In the case of earthquakes, if the various points of access are not re-established in a short enough time to keep active these mediating links which constitute control points, there can be a weakening on the Lines, also because there are Minor Lines which are linked together.

A Minor Line, once created, is maintained by the Major Lines. The energy that maintains it cannot therefore be annulled: there can be difficulties in the manipulation of this energy, the access to a Minor Line can be blocked, but blocking an access does not mean that the Minor Line has been impaired or shut down.

If the entry to a Minor Line is damaged, it will however take a long time to re-open, since this involves a very complicated operation.

These accesses must be in a meeting point between the physical and the non-physical realms. Only in the case of very serious disturbances will there be a risk of the Minor Lines being damaged.

THE KNOTS FORMED
BY THE MINOR LINES

T o be able to be used, the Synchronic Lines must form knots, which are extremely rare and very important. We are not looking at knots originating from the meeting of the great general Lines, but at places close to the points of flow: the 18 general Lines do not touch directly, each one follows its own way down through the millennia.

On the maps of the Synchronic Lines there can be Lines that seem to touch while they only come close without crossing each other.

89

In several cases the points which seem overlapping are far away from each other and beyond each other's reach. Furthermore the maps are drawn with different proportions and at times the points end up not shown in their exact position. When the Lines touch it means that Minor Lines have been created or that one has Minor Lines capable of making a link: let us remember that we also need to take into account the Lines far below and high above the point under consideration.

Imagine that the point where the shortest distance from one Minor Line to another is point A, there will be one Minor Line (1) which comes from one direction,

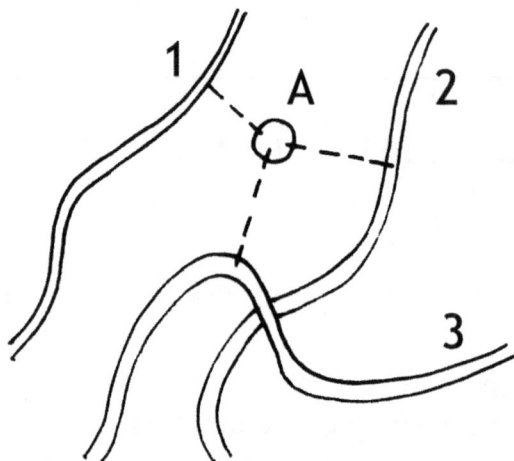

Nodes connecting a Minor Line to three Major Lines.

then another (2) which comes from another direction, then a third still (3).

Linked up in this way, the Minor Lines will carry out their function. Taking a look in particular at the combination of the knot of Lines found where the Temples

Geometries formed by Minor nodes.

of Humankind are situated, we see that here there is an intricate series of links of Minor Lines to Minor Lines.

Compared to the exact position of the points previously touched, today there are links that go much further afield, a series of Minor Lines that create a shape forming a rough triangle and a series of superimposed internal links.

This means that every General Line can under certain conditions be capable of supporting an increased number of Minor Lines.

91

Complex geometries formed by Minor Line nodes.

Having the capacity, one could theoretically create more channels; this means using much more energy because the amount of energy is proportional to the connections. Over the whole of this area there are a series of Minor connections that are then linked, co-ordinated, in particular by utilising selfic installations.

Imagine we have a series of links and connections between these points via a system developed in the last
few years using spheroself technology and co-ordinating
and modifying the structuring of Northern Italy with regard to the installations and the flow of the Lines.

The shining knot of this geographical location, the
site of the Temples of Humankind, is thus in reality composed of several knots with different types of
connections.

In fact where knots are formed they can have an influence on people for many centuries; indeed, when made
proper use of, they can have an influence on the successive incarnations of the creatures living near the knot.

Research has shown that within the space of a few
years, the synchronic knots can shift toward areas where
new centres of knowledge are to arise. And it is there
that huge potentials are created: they are the Forces
which have been used for centuries and millennia in
Tibet, India, Egypt and Central America.

The people of antiquity managed to keep active contacts of great importance.

At Stonehenge, in the South of England, Minor Lines
were built which still today, if used under the right conditions, permit control of the Forces produced by the
major Lines.

And in antiquity, as we have said, accessible places
where two or more Synchronic Lines met, were the chosen sites for the central areas of the temples – these being the priests' "laboratories".

The most important civilisations of the past have flourished at the meeting points of the Lines.

With the passing of the millennia the Lines have tended to shift very slowly towards the north, while the synchronic knots - which in different times may be more or less active - move much more quickly: you could say they dart about. For example, the most important energies and their surfacing points, which up to 2,500 - 3,000 years ago flowed in particular through Egypt and the area of the Middle East, have shifted northwards.

The surfacing points tend to be more numerous where the different Lines are closer together. To be able to utilise this energy it is not enough to come in contact with a Line, various elements are needed. In particular it requires that the stream be within our physical reach (that is not far underground or at the bottom of the sea or too high in the sky), and it must be at a meeting point with another Line, a knot.

When we refer to the Minor Lines, we talk about the knots as a point of balance between two Minor Lines which have neutralised one another: the reciprocal pressures in that point are equal to zero.

Thus Knots are the point where further insertions are possible. When a Minor Line is formed, what happens on one side is mirrored on the other side: if one of the Minor Lines rises up, the other too must rise, if one moves down, the other too will move down as a result, in mirror-image fashion. Therefore a great deal of time is needed for special Lines like this to be formed.

93

Minor Lines created by the will of man can attach to these knots. Particular links can be made at times by utilising sections already in existence, by making use of the Earth magnetic Lines, or by superimposing Minor Lines, or networks of Minor Lines, onto telluric Lines.

DESCRIPTION OF THE TYPES OF MINOR LINES AND THEIR USE

T he Minor Lines are Minor in name but certainly not in importance. Let us give them numerical values for reference so as to have an idea of their practical use. When used in the appropriate place, the two opposite spirals of the Minor Lines meld, giving birth to a Line of a particular colour, straight as a pencil.

The Minor Lines change their type, i.e. their colour and value on the basis of the types of meetings they make. As the torrent of energy gradually becomes lesser, they are distinguished also by colour, above all when a Red (or Vertical) Line approaches a Blue (Horizontal) one.

According to the type and number of the Lines that meet, a mathematical value has been assigned linked to a colour.

- The Minor Lines formed from the meeting of two Red Lines are green and have the value 12.
- A meeting between a Red and a Blue Line produces a Violet Line with a value of 24 – a value of 24 that is identified with the colour violet.
- Those derived from two Red and a Blue are White and have a value of 48 (for example a White Line comes from the meeting of the Second, the Third and Line D off the coast of South America).

95

- Two Blue Lines when they meet up make a Yellow and have a value of 91.
- The Lines derived from two Blue and a Red are Golden and have a value of 182.
- Two Blue and two Red Lines give rise to the Shining Lines and have a value of 365. Only two cases are known, one in Europe (where Damanhur now stands, editor's note) and one in Tibet.

In antiquity Line D ran further north, through North Africa (including Egypt). It was the age of the great pyramids, superbly activated at the time.

The great researchers who had ancient knowledge often used energies catalysed from several Green or Violet Lines to gradually spark off greater effects. By preparing the right formulae, in the form of chalices, or mirrors of energy, one can give form to this output (generally triangles are projected), starting from one or several Minor Lines.

Where Lines reflecting one another meet (for example two Green Lines) special inter-penetrating fields are created. On those points, and inside these forms, whoever has total knowledge of the laws which govern this universe may, for controlled evolutionary purposes, evoke entities, daemons, forms, Forces, souls and, if the energies are appropriate and well combined, do so with infinite precision, triggering astounding alchemical processes.

In these cases selfic technology helps a great deal.

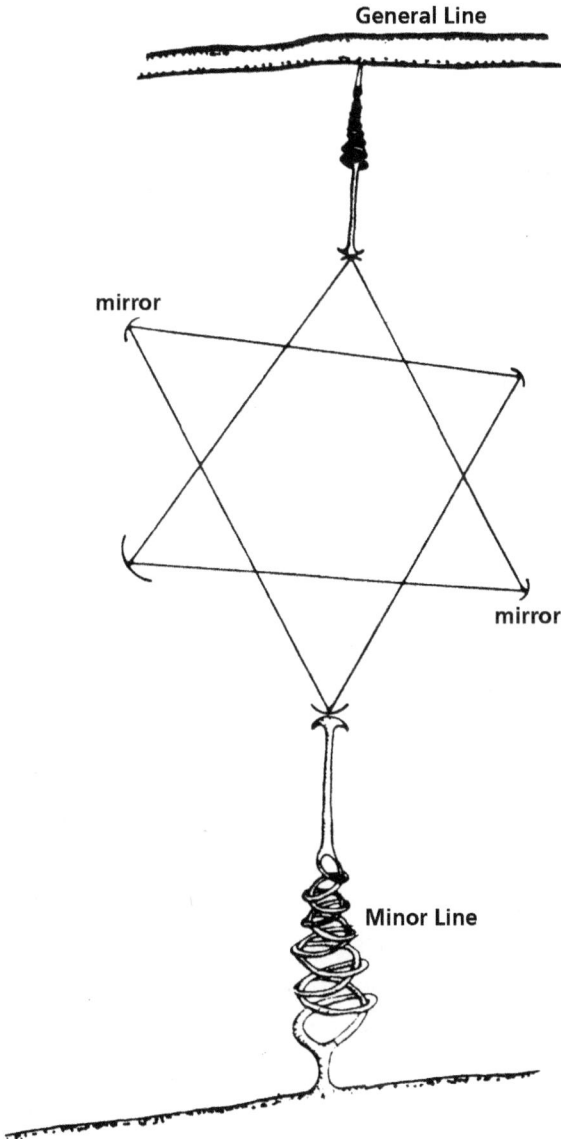

General Line

mirror

mirror

97

Minor Line

*The mirrors (chalices of energy) are
utilised in contacting the Minor Lines.*

Thanks to such technology it is possible to construct lines much more easily than in the past. The selfic systems of great complexity now replace the building of cathedrals which served to create the Minor Lines.

Then thousands of people were needed for hundreds of years, but now it is possible to do the same in a much shorter period of time. The "fuel" used in these operations is the same as the energy being extracted – like having a well that draws out much more oil than is needed to make the pump work.

In order to get close and better utilise the Minor Lines with appropriate technology, a sort of aqueduct is required to carry the energies where they are needed. To be able to utilise the Minor Lines in fact requires a considerable amount of psychic energy, and much more so if the Minor Line has a high value.

The consumption of psychic energies needed here can be truly immense: it could equal the emotional charge generated by the whole of the First and Second World Wars put together, or the power of prayer of millions of faithful for centuries and centuries: it is thus evident that it is important to be close to these synchronic surfacing points, to avoid this task of transferring energy where what is consumed can be greater than what is gained.

To utilise these portals accessing such huge Forces, it is thus worth the effort of digging, sculpting, climbing, building, travelling, flying – whatever is needed.

One could also, with the right knowledge, use ancient temples apparently fallen into disuse to trigger off such

Forces, but at a considerable risk: it would be a case of making astral journeys and carrying out séances, mobilising entities and even divinities.

Let us hypothesise that anyone who could succeed in triggering a process by means of the Minor Lines, becoming capable of utilising the Golden Lines or perhaps even the Shining Lines, would be able to achieve other things that have all the flavour of high science fiction: they could travel to and from parallel worlds, act synchronically by entering into the desired North-South or East-West streams by means of the distribution of the Minor Lines which connect the whole worldwide network.

Above all they could start appropriate operations to create historical changes causing a new evolutionary leap for humankind. To realise such a far-reaching objective one would have to make suitable things happen at the right time and in the right place.

99

It is a matter of giving and receiving information by entering into such an immense circuit at almost infinite speeds and opposite spiral antennae to the north and south.

Whoever has such grandiose knowledge is capable of talking on a level with the most evolved beings of the galaxy and of carrying the voice of humanity to the stars.

THE SYNCHRONIC LINES IN INDIA, TIBET, NEPAL

Some mountains for example in India, Tibet, Nepal, (home of so many spiritual paths) are variable antennas and it is therefore interesting to note their influence on the surrounding area, especially when they are touched by Major Lines.

Since Minor Lines that form in this area are, as we shall soon see, really numerous (their value amounts to seven hundred ninety-nine, that we know of), these are places that are eminently suitable for many magic operations .

101

Tibet exploited these possibilities, throughout its history, creating "mystical aqueducts" to divert the lines in order to fully utilize this power.

Along the Himalayas, the two Major Red lines, the Seventh and the Eighth, meet each other no less than seven times creating as many Minor Lines, value of 12 green.

Also two Red and one Blue, forming a White with a value of 48, plus two Blue and one Red forming a Golden 182, two Blue and two Red which give a Shining value of 365 and also a Red and a Blue (at least five times) constituting a purple 24.

On average, every hundred Km there are at least six natural Minor Lines, amidst rivers, mountains, and physical locations like those at issue.

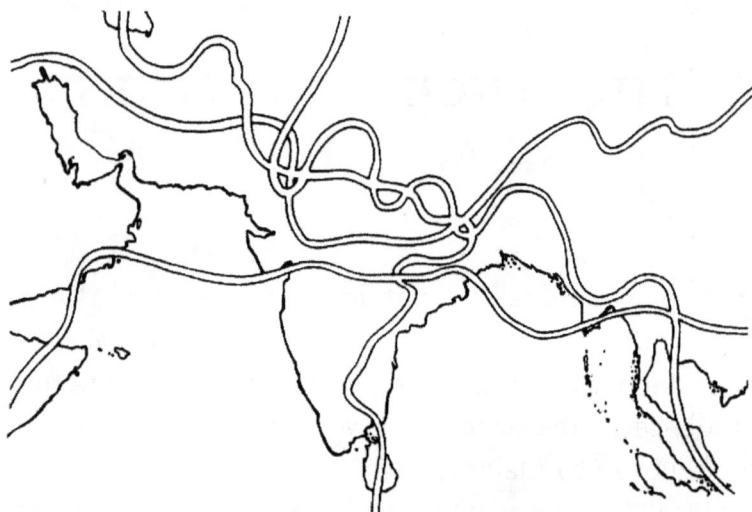

Special patterning of the Lines in India-Tibet-Nepal.

So over the 1,500 km (the length of the area in question) there are no less than ninety opportunities, that is a power of 71,910, which means 197 occasions for a Shining Knot.

To be able to assemble and maintain so many Forces in a balanced relationship between them, there is essential consumption, calculated by dividing the number by three.

The result is sixty-six Shining Knots via which it is possible to produce drawings, pentacles, magical spirals that can predetermine rebirths and influence the world over distances of centuries and millennia, produce and project synchronic Forces on any line and emerge through the Minors at any place on Earth.

However, the great Indo-Tibetan Forces are, in this so-called Aquarian Age, moving to other major hubs.

In order to properly use such great energy, sometimes operators produce nodes in deep caves without physical entrances. Such places are only reachable by those who have the knowledge, that is, by Wizards.

Evidently it is not enough to know how to leave the physical body. These places, well watched over as they are by guards and shielded from energies are reachable only by those who have the strength, the presence and the preparation.

One could thus imagine that the various myths recounting journeys to the Underworld, like the descent of Christ into Hell, the *Divine Comedy* of Dante (with Charon to meet, rivers to cross, tests to overcome, Pluto the guardian) are in reality popular representations of this knowledge, unbeknownst to most and thus esoteric.

The immense power conferred on those who know how to reach these mystic places has earned them the name of Lords of Karma. Such a term indicates that these are beings capable of changing – by using the law of synchronicity – the values of action (karma means action) according to justice presided over by higher Forces.

Such wonderful places preserve everything that the human being (not limiting this to our physical form) has done, written, thought in thousands of years, perhaps in hundreds of thousands of years...

These are after all the real doorways, stargates to the universe. Forget about spaceships!

THE SURFACING OF
THE SYNCHRONIC LINES
IN EUROPE

When the Mediterranean was the centre of the world, Europe and Africa were the two sides. Millennium after millennium, from Egypt, from the Middle East, the Lines of the dragon's back have shifted more and more towards the North-West. The Lines passed through Sicily, moved up the sea, then began to become dense around the places that later on were to become "special" cities, as we shall see.

In Europe there are several Minor Lines which have great importance. In ancient times several civilisations constructed what is a really exceptional monument from a magical point of view: the Minor Line joining Paris and Prague, such that it forms a triangle with its apex in Turin.

This work which joined two major Lines was begun by the Druid priesthood: after learning the knowledge from other peoples including from the Egyptians. They succeeded in carrying out such an extremely important, monumental, task that it will last for centuries to come. The groups that later looked after this work limited themselves to carrying out maintenance, keeping the surfacing points in order.

To build, using the laws of magic, a very powerful Minor Line is a grandiose task indeed from a magical point of view.

Many temples have been built on sites close to Minor Lines in the past, in order to keep some of these Lines active. To have control of a particular area, it is essential to have the contact points with these Forces at one's disposal.

In Europe four Lines meet: two general Red and two general Blue Lines (A and B).

In twelve points they overlap one another: Line A and the Fifth on the isle of Grimsey, right on the Arctic Circle, near the Icelandic coast (violet 24).

A simple surfacing happens on Britain's isle of Rockall, with the Fifth Red Line, but it is of little value even though it is stable, while another violet 24 Line meeting occurs about 125 miles to the north-west of Ireland: but the Minor Lines are formed a little below sea level and are not therefore easy to make use of.

The situation is different in Ireland, near Mount Carrantuohill, to the west of Cork, because Blue Line A flows just a few dozen metres – less than a hundred feet – above the ground.

Almost the whole of Ireland is surrounded by a ring made up of Line A and the Fifth and since even the Fifth also surfaces, roughly following the border between Northern and Southern Ireland, fields of not intense but diffuse Minor Lines are created (several violet 24).

The Fifth Red Line passes through Mount Snowdon in North Wales and meets Blue Line A again - but this time surfacing in points that are very close - near Gloucester in the West of England (six violet 24).

Line A follows the coast of Wales running east just north of Cardiff, only barely surfacing there (a few miles away we have three violet 24). The line then turns north-east towards Norwich (one violet 24) before crossing the North Sea in the direction of Amsterdam.

Let us assign a conventional value to the simple sur-facings, of 3 or 6 according to their ability to be utilised and the distance between two general Lines.

The Fifth surfaces several more times as far as the Isle of Wight (six times, equals approximately 24) before crossing the Channel at a depth, at times crossing great caverns as far as Chartres where it surfaces several times with a certain intensity (6-6-6), and turns towards Paris where there too it comes out onto the surface.

Here there was created one of the most impressive monuments of the occult world: a very ancient Minor Line, made masterly use of by Nostradamus, Cornelius Agrippa, Cagliostro and other magicians. It was "built" by the Celts and other peoples and restored in more re-cent times by the early Ritual Egyptian Freemasonry with the help of the Rosicrucians, the Templars and other se-cret orders.

It is a channel fully 600 miles (900 kilometres) long: a very strong Minor Line that joins Paris and Prague, passing through Rheims, brushing Luxembourg, and on to Mannheim, Nuremberg and Pilsen. This is in fact the greatest Minor Line in the world.

Many European churches, temples and sanctuaries served as triggers with the purpose of maintaining this Line.

This Minor Line winds three times around Line A almost under the Rhine, near Mannheim and from this Blue Line, it "extracts" other Minor Lines which allow one to activate the following:

- Red (Paris) Blue (Mannheim) - violet 24
- Blue (Mannheim) Blue (Prague) - yellow 91
- Blue (Mannheim) Red (Prague) - violet 24
- Red (Paris) Red (Prague) green 12
- all multiplied by three.

Let us return to Blue Line A, which from Amsterdam crosses very high over the Low Countries (to coin a phrase!), passes through Essen, Cologne (a Minor Line) and, following the Rhine, reaches Mannheim. From here it heads for the mountains, towards Stuttgart, reaches and passes beyond the Danube and arrives in Switzerland where it surfaces almost vertically near Zurich, just touches Berne and heads for the Italian Alps and Monte Rosa.

Meanwhile, the Fifth Red Line carries on its way from Paris to Troyes, following the Seine for a while, and surfacing a few times near Mâcon as far as Lyons. From Lyons (where several Minor Lines meet with Line B, all with a violet value of 24) it heads towards Mont Blanc making, with Line B, a kind of funnel pointing down towards Italy.

The Blue Line is that Line on the dragon's back which enters eastward Europe, after putting in an appearance in the Azores, passes through Cape St. Vincent, the most westerly point of Portugal, and flows through the Sierra Morena in Spain, to surface in Toledo, then near present-day Madrid. From there it goes to Tornel, before re-appearing close to Barcelona and running on into the Mediterranean.

From here, just over a mile underground, it goes back up the Rhone and re-emerges at Grenoble (but passing very high above it) and comes close, as already mentioned, to the Fifth Red Line making the kind of funnel shape we mentioned, and so into Italy, running from Montgenevre, passing by Frejus, and on towards Bardonecchia.

Then, after passing through Italy, the Blue Line touches Austria at Salzburg, brushes Linz and heads towards Prague. There we find one of the most curious of the shapes made by the Synchronic Lines, creating a funnel corridor 750 miles (1,200 kilometres) long.

The Force accumulated by these great Lines, the natural channels of the journey along the main lines of energy as far as Italy, are a significant Force channelled into the Canavese (northern Italy, above Turin, where Damanhur is situated).

Let us follow Line A again: we had followed it as far as Italy. From there it moves up into Poland, crosses Bydgoszcz and comes out in the sea near Elbiag, on the Baltic; it then moves back into Lithuania to the south of Ventspils and then plunges back into the sea, passes into Estonia by Tartu and, fifty kilometres or so (thirty miles) south of St. Petersburg, it meets the Sixth once more (which it had followed for 750 miles from Italy to Poland).

Going back with the Sixth in the opposite direction, we see that from Prague it goes into Poland near Lennica and breaks surface again to head for Lodz and Warsaw.

Then it runs through Russia in the direction of Minsk, surfaces markedly at Orsa, continues across the Steppes surfacing only twice as it turns in the direction of Moscow, heads towards Novgorod and finally after its meeting with Line A reaches St. Petersburg.

From here it skirts the western side of Lake Ladozskoje, moves into Finland to the north of Helsinki, surfaces near Tampere and then turns decisively northward, among rivers, lakes, mountains, rarely surfacing.

Line A meanwhile, having passed 30 miles (50 kilometres) to the south of Petersburg, reaches Ukhta surfacing only twice on the way and having crossed the Urals along the Pecora river, it moves into Asia.

The Sixth Red Line, from Italy brushes Olbia, passes through the Aeolian Islands, crosses the Straits of Messina and turns into the Ionian Sea moving into Greece almost following the boundary with Albania.

Line B moves into ex-Yugoslavia to the north of Albania, surface by Skpoje, passes into Macedonia; from the mountains of Greece there issues an important Minor Line, presently in complete disuse, which after bushing Blue Line B, also brushes the Sixth Red Line in Macedonia surfacing six times (several violet 24) heading for Olympus (some 60 miles to the south): one of these Minor Lines, massive and powerful, instead heads east towards Mount Athos.

From this point the Sixth Red Line surfaces (or comes down) on a couple of little islands in the Aegean, before touching the vaults in Istanbul, crossing the Bosphorus and continuing into Asia.

Blue Line B itself, after the bottleneck between Macedonia and Greece, crosses Bulgaria, passes through Plovdiv, moves into Romania a few miles from the sea surfacing several times, and near Constanta it crosses the Black Sea reaching the Caucasus.

TERRESTRIAL ISLANDS, TERRESTRIAL PLATES, "ARROWHEAD ISLANDS" AND OTHER LINES ON THE PLANET

T he areas encircled by major Lines are called terrestrial islands. They are of particular interest in this field of research: the smaller the area enclosed by the Lines, the more important its function.

We have spoken of "funnels", like that formed to the west of the Fifth Red Line as it runs from Paris to Lyon and on to Turin, and by Blue Line B in its Madrid-Barcelona -(Lyons)-Turin stretch.

The Forces enclosed within the Lines are literally funnelled towards the "neck" of the funnel, the apex of the triangle. Let us now look at the European terrestrial islands.

- ISLAND A: an area of Ireland, theoretical value 100.
- ISLAND B: London-Paris-Amsterdam (along the Minor Paris-Prague Line). This is the sole example of a constructed island, value 60.
- ISLAND C: with the 75 mile (120 km) funnel directed towards the Canavese area of Piedmont, North West Italy, triangle value (excluding the funnel) 40.

113

- ISLANDS D-E: One of the three golden islands comprising the celebrated Turin-Paris-Prague triangle. We give D the value 100 and the same for E. The particular conformation of the great Line A with its sharply acute angle as it turns toward Italy, almost creates a funnel.
- ISLAND F: comprises the Prague-Turin corridor, closed by the last miles of the Minor Line (violet 24) between the Sixth and Line A. Value 300.
- ISLAND G-H-I-L: are the smallest, therefore of the greatest value. Whoever manages to use them, mostly combined among themselves is fortunate indeed. We give a value 2,400.
- ISLAND M: is really more of a corridor than an island. Value 100.
- ISLAND N: a balanced island, almost the mirror of the Irish one (island A). Value??
- ISLAND O: the mirror of the natural one that would be formed by B + D. Value 60. Really it is open but in the past was considered closed by the Minor Olympus-Macedonia Line.
- ISLAND P: is the biggest European island, Sicily is its tip. Value 40.
- ISLAND Q: is the Icelandic-Atlantic island. Value 30. It has never been used.

At great depths, 30 miles or more beneath the surface, there are "shields", or energy vortices, which project their Forces upwards. These are the terrestrial plates.

These shields are fed by the great Synchronic Lines and act like a sort of deposit, to keep the Forces always in balance.

One of these plates is situated in Denmark and Sweden and takes power from Line A (with one corner touching the Faeroe islands), from the Sixth Line near Tampere, and also north of Berlin. Let us now see what the arrowhead islands are.

As already mentioned, the great north-south Lines can be utilised for no more than 3-4% of their course. But from this percentage we have to take away the places that are difficult to travel to, such as the North Pole and the icy wastes of the South Pole, parts of Siberia, or where Lines are too high in the sky or on mountains difficult to access. Thus the isolated points where different Lines surface or are projected into the sky become extremely important: like terrestrial islands emerging from the seas.

Let us first of all talk about the European islands of particular interest.

The Fifth surfaces on the island of Rockall, to the north of Ireland, where it meets violet 24, a Minor Line coming from Blue Line A.

To the south, in the Tyrrhenian Sea, past Sardinia, there is a point where the Fifth surfaces amid the Aegadi islands, to the west of Marsala, in Sicily; and then soon afterwards it surfaces in Malta, where it so to speak slices through a Minor from the Sixth off the coast of Catania.

Then there are three emerging points on the island of Crete, with its complicated configuration as if the island had at some time been shrivelled and squashed.

It is likely that these Earth movements were caused by events in the past probably of a volcanic nature. There were perhaps other islands linked with Crete or possibly it formed one bigger or differently shaped island. Thus important geological movements too can be deduced from the Lines.

The Sixth surfaces first in Sardinia and then on the island of Corfu and then again near Lyndos and on certain rocky outcrops in the Aegean.

Taking a look at the rest of the world we note that the First Red Line surfaces in Hawaii; here there is a temple cavern[1], partly open to the sky. Ideally this phenomenon could have a 360° range of action and undoubtedly functions can manifest within it: the tube so formed can be stretched, take other shapes, come to the surface of the sea; it has a part that emerges to form a kind of bubble, which exists courtesy of a Minor Line.

The First Red Line then crosses the Equator, where it alters the influence of the constellations, to re-appear in Polynesia, in the Society Islands . To say that a Line alters the influence of the constellations means that there are astrological influences from the stars, and that this influence at the moment of birth is altered by the presence of the line. This is a peculiarity that holds for all the Lines and is the starting point for a new way of understanding astrology, taking into consideration these variables in addition to the traditional ones.

After touching Cuba and a few rocky islets in the Caribbean, the Second Line re-appears with remarkable

Force in the Galapagos, where it meets the Third line and Blue Line D (White 48).

Almost on the Tropic of Capricorn, it meets the Third again, for the last time – on the sea-bed, or rather, on the peak of a great underwater mountain sloping towards Easter Island. Here another great oddity happens: besides the formation of at least three White 48, the Blue Line acts like a Minor Line and runs as far as Easter Island where it sheds its load in an opposite direction to the normal current running from east to west.

The fact that the Blue acts as a Minor Line can be understood as follows: it is as if it were a great mine forming now, in our time, at a faster rate than the normal time for the formation of a mine (which generally takes tens of millions of years). When a whole Line carries out the functions of a Minor Line, it means it has an exit into form, it is not limited to circulating round the planet: in such a case perhaps it will manage to form a mine in a mere thousand or two thousand years.

The Third Line, after touching several of the islands in the Bahamas, produces the same phenomenon as Line F, and does so with Line C off Bermuda, where it becomes a plate rather than a Line, moving in the opposite direction.

However, having crossed Hispaniola (Haiti), Jamaica, and Barbados, it runs into the Pacific, where it is not seen again southward until the tip of Cape Horn.

117

[1] Temple caverns are a kind of bubble where everything is surrounded, encompassed, regardless of its contents. It could be likened to a tube that is inflated and maintains stretches of land, water, or any other substance intact within it.

THE OVAL LINES

O n the planet Earth besides the Synchronic Lines and the Minor Lines there are also the Oval Lines, so called, logically enough, because they are oval in cross section. Their size varies depending on the measurements of the Minor Lines. The oval Lines are surface Lines; to access them one has above all to be tuned in to such energies.

In Europe as in other parts of the world the oval Lines were used and travelled for millennia by many different populations; in Europe it was easier to utilise them in conjunction with complex constructions (like Stonehenge or other sites in Britain and France) where the Forces of the Oval Lines were orientated using the placement of the structures. Such sites also took on a spiritual function, of contact with the divine Forces.

In some places on the Earth there are concentrations of these Oval Lines: being soft they can be modified and manipulated, unlike the Synchronic Lines which cannot be modified. They can be travelled along and otherwise utilised. They allow Forces to be concentrated. Behaving somewhat as if they were little sisters of the Synchronic Lines, they may be used to act on the latter and direct Forces for specific uses. Once they were manipulated in a way that would make it easier to contact the Minor Lines.

These Oval Lines are always linked to the Synchronic Lines, but at times they form very long chains perhaps in places distant from the Synchronic Lines.

Often their path is influenced by the position of *menhirs* and *dolmens,* as we have seen. The practical use of the Oval Lines is to concentrate events. Being linked to synchronicity they are able to condense synchronic events in relation to the stones' size and weight. Their position can be shifted with reference to masses just as iron filings are moved into a pattern around a magnet: the stones become a sort of lens for underlying energies and are positioned on the basis of precise mathematical relationships.

These energetic configurations, then, are often situated close to ancient artefacts. The ancient peoples of Europe placed many standing stones of different sizes where they identified natural surfacing points of the Lines: arrangements of very large stones have in the past allowed the collection of energies composed of non-substance substance.

In the South of France there are many *menhirs*, (standing stones) indicating the presence of numerous Oval Lines linked to each other. The original populations here and elsewhere had close contact with all that was primeval. They harkened to the voices of time and space and were very close to the dream reality, so much so that they found it difficult to distinguish the dream state from the real.

MAGNETIC (OR TELLURIC) LINES AND SYNCHRONIC AND A-SYNCHRONIC POINTS

T here are terrestrial Lines that have nothing to do with the Synchronic Lines, known as Telluric (or Magnetic) Lines. These can be indicative of nega- tive or positive conditions, of health or sickness, on aver- age they are about one cubit wide – an ancient Egyptian measurement[1]. These lines flow exclusively underground and carry intense magnetic fields that can produce such disturbances as to induce madness in certain cases.

On the planet Earth there are a very large number of telluric lines, some produce positive effects, others neg- ative ones, but it is difficult for anyone to succeed in shielding themselves from these influences; at certain times these effects are increased by foreseeable plan- etary influences. The whole of the Earth is encompassed by these telluric lines surfacing like capillaries, which may be fluctuating and in certain places they may be particularly concentrated.

On average every 70 inches (1.8) metres, lines of this type intersect, so that they form a grid: in a room there could be four or five positive places and as many nega- tive ones: taken as a whole they generally balance one another.

121

By dowsing, knowing the frequency one is looking for, one can trace and identify the points where they are present, noting whether they are positive or negative and whether they are especially active.

A graphic example of the telluric lines issue is Vercelli in Northern Italy, where two Minor Lines pass near the city, in addition to a telluric line – not a very pleasant one – which runs underground. A line of this kind can weigh on the life of an area, creating nervousness and tension.

When the intense astral influence of the full moon is added to this factor, quite heavy corresponding effects can be noticed. And in general, for example, there are roads which while not being particularly dangerous are the scene of very many accidents.

These are usually at crossroads which at first sight are more or less like any other. But if they coincide with a telluric line of this nature, they can contribute to making the driver distracted.

Before building houses, too, we should do well to check out the terrain to avoid places where there would likely be problems, tension, insomnia. At times one cannot manage to sleep well in a room until the bed is moved. Where there is a particular combination of underground streams, this would have to be dealt with by a very complex operation to deviate the surfacing points by at least a few metres. It's also possible to set up a defence by employing complex selfic devices.

Many animals have the ability to sense these places, for example cats: cats choose to sleep in places that would not be suitable for human beings. In this regard Dogs too have good sensitivity.

And regarding the Synchronic Lines, notice that as well as synchronic places there are also a-synchronic places, which balance them out. There is a fall of events, a rain of neutral, uncoloured events that falls every fraction of time. This rain ends up in a stream that is orientated in relation to the Synchronic Lines.

By *a-synchronic* points we mean locations where there remains a residue of unused events. It is as if the Synchronic Lines bore fruit like a walnut for example and the negative residue left behind would be the shell, just to give an example. We cannot talk of about a-synchronic lines as such, but we are looking at a series of events which have experienced a deviation which is essentially like the opposite or downside of the fruit: neither the shell nor the kernel are then edible.

123

Take the case of people who live close to points corresponding to "kernels", generally fluctuating points, in movement, which represent veritable time storms. At times they can be identified on the edges of those peculiarities we call White Lines (see below, editor's note) because in those areas events happen in particularly synchronic fashion to produce effects: it is like saying there is more water in a cloud compared to the environment around it.

Thus mental illness can derive from a confusion of events and that hence one is no longer able to distinguish what is called reality from fantasy because they are two realities side by side and one is living with one foot in both of them.

In antiquity the women of particularly evolved peoples used to give birth in selected places, always somewhere different from their previous births, so as to avoid their little one taking on the same "destiny matrix" as others already born: this on the basis of the principal that if the child is born in the proper place, it will be linked to the telluric Forces of the place in addition to having the influences of the cosmic Forces of that moment (from whose study astrology is derived).

---

[1] Cubit: a measurement used in Ancient Egypt and elsewhere. The distance between elbow and middle finger, Two types of cubit were used, the small cubit measuring 44.7 cm (18 inches) in every day use, and the architects' cubit, measuring 52.5 cm (20.8 inches).

SYNCHRONIC LINES, SPHERES AND SELFIC DEVICES

The network of spheroselfs works in an integrated manner together with the Synchronic Lines: The selfs and the spheroselfs are structures that work symbiotically with the person they have been prepared for. Spheroselfs can act as an amplifier, amplifying the signal. Thanks to selfica it is possible to use even Minor Lines far from our entrance point. In addition, the selfic network allows us to prevent access to the Synchronic Lines by other Forces, or else to have more entrance points to send a given message correctly.

125

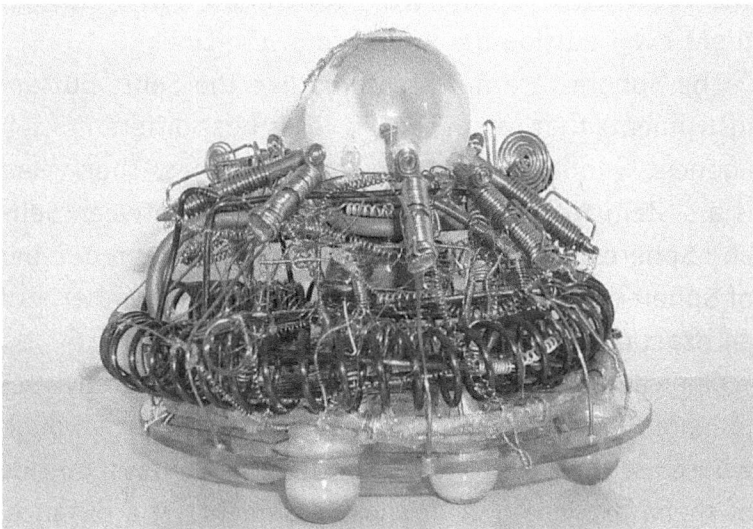

Thanks to this, it is possible to recover a message that has been stuck somewhere along the Line: this is what we call a "chessboard reaction".

A personal Self, amplified also by a Spheroself, can act on the Synchronic Lines if there is a specific link. Access codes are always needed in using the various appropriate systems, but there has to be a possible opening.

And indeed, use of particular Spheres in the Temples of Humankind in Damanhur permits access to the Synchronic Lines. The Spheroselfs do not act directly on the system of the Lines but act in relation to the Spheres *in situ*: the reference starting point is hence a sphere.

126

The Spheres themselves are technology linked to the selfic copper devices. Thanks to the latter, it is possible to multiply the effects, act in places and environments within which it is otherwise difficult to move – sometimes even outside the influence of the Lines.

The Spheres are not creatures like the Selfs, but are instruments that can in certain cases host different intelligences, very different from the selfic ones. Then there is a system to create a kind of symbiosis between Selfs and Spheres. On this planet there is a maximum number of Spheres that can be used: not an infinite number, but an exact one.

One can imagine the spheres as bowls of different sizes prepared with alchemical liquids, containers through whose use it is possible to act on the Lines or even outside of them, examining or producing elements at a distance, giving and receiving information or more specialised elements. One can think of the Sphere as a sort of cam-recorder that can be placed anywhere on the planet.

There are however security systems to filter out possible errors. The access codes to enter a Synchronic Line are similar to those for a computer; they must be used opportunely and responsibly: if errors are made the sphere in use is deactivated and to re-charge it and prepare it again will take a lot of time. We cannot take it for granted that the structure can be kept permanently functioning.

With the sphere systems it is possible to influence events through the Synchronic Lines to the extent of even producing physical events. However one has to pay infinite attention in using Forces that can be used to vary time, to modify cloud movements or to modify the rate of absorption of a mass of water. There is also need of spaces and places to discharge these energies.

One operates on the Lines by introducing information which passes through the points of access, the appropriate points where these gateways exist. Information is sent and received on the Lines which can change the behaviour of animals, plants, human beings.

Clashes and wars have happened over the: whoever acts on them finds themselves fighting enemies who cover areas of strategic importance inhabited by human beings.

The access to the Synchronic Lines involves going through very complex and well-protected passages between levels of energy.

127

Therefore to send information one needs Forces, creatures, highly specialised beings which have the ability to access the different planes of existence, from our real one to others still, through which it would be possible to return onto our plane of existence bringing events with them. The Lines, roads formed by life, not only diffuse energies over the planet but souls transit along them as we have said. Along these privileged roads pass other spiritual forms too, such as the souls of the species or of melding of species. These roads are strengthened thanks to the very contribution of the beings that travel them.

We can see our relationship with the creatures of selfic origin who belong to a "meta-world" in contact with ours: the Forces that go to dwell inside the self come from this 'meta-world' and transmigrate into ours.

There is a limit to what can be introduced onto the Lines; this will vary on the basis of combinations that are to do with the alchemy of living Forces, i.e. the combination of energies, emotions, elements produced by living beings.

When the spheres are utilised, the type of intensity of the request for intervention may change. It is one thing to send signals, elements to be modified and diffused in another part of the world over the Lines, and something else to request through them the participation of major Forces which will then intervene through or even outside of the Lines themselves: whoever knows how to master techniques of this kind can multiply the type of influence they exert a hundredfold.

THE SYNCHRONIC LINES AND THE TEMPLES OF HUMANKIND

D amanhur stands on a major knot of Lines, as we have seen, and Damanhur's Temples of Humankind have been built exactly where it was possible to reach the point where the Lines surfaced.

In this area the energetic fields are markedly different from other places on Earth, as has also been testified by the studies and the samples taken by the geologists who have analysed the sub-strata and the surrounding land where it was built.

The main part of the Temple of Humankind, the Hall of Mirrors, is in fact perfectly placed in a rare band of

129

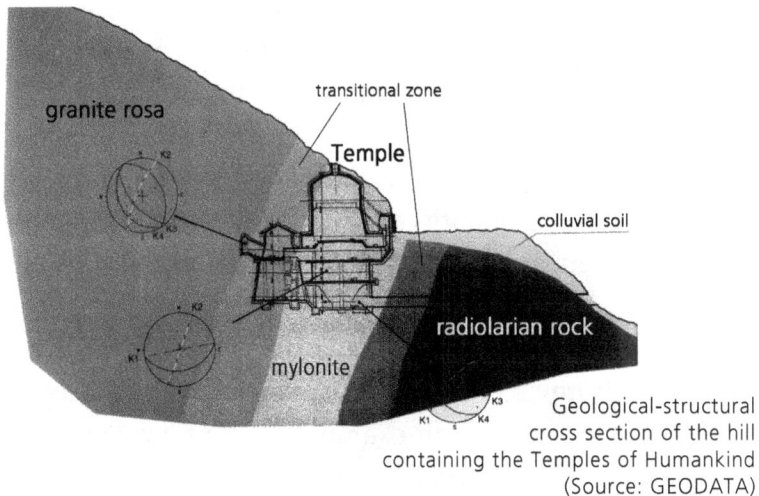

Geological-structural cross section of the hill containing the Temples of Humankind (Source: GEODATA)

a mineral especially charged with energy because it was formed during the colliding of the continents. As one can read in an excerpt from a geology report: «In the area of the Temples of Humankind various minerals are found amongst which mylonite: this is a multi-layer, dark-looking rock with very fine pale layers, including white. In many cases along the bands of this material we can see the emergence of deeper materials. Precisely as a consequence of the qualities described, the rock formations formed by mylonite are characterised by possible energy flows of notable intensity».

The volume, the space, the thickness of the rock in the Temples of Humankind are constituted so as to make best use of the energy of the Synchronic Lines.

According to studies made in Damanhur, the Temples also constitute a time mine[1]. Near the Lines or along their stream there are mines of events, as we see precisely in the Temples of Humankind. Events manifest in form the moment they are extracted: for example two particles create a phenomenon in the moment when they meet, but not until then.

A more intense flowing of the current, in this case synchronic, brings a quantity of events that have not manifested but are merely attracted. This faculty of "unused weight" in the long run stratifies and remains on one side with the possibility of influencing other objects in their synchronicity: nothing is destroyed, even what is not deployed.

One can imagine as an example – albeit limited – that any collapse in the form of objects touched by the Lines, can become a stratification of neutral events (events not yet realised): then something can happen through natural causes (volcanic action for example) or through the intervention of living forms (complexity). This Planet in fact moves significantly: it collapses, rises, shifts, does all kind of things, even if we do not realise because this happens over thousands of years.

To make the time mines work, energies must be made to pass through mass, as happens with a magnet when an electric current is passed through a piece of metal to give the energy an alignment, or orientation. With the same system it is possible to give orientation to a gradually greater and greater physical mass: a cubic kilometre of earth has a infinitesimal mass in comparison with the planet, but the moment it receives an orientation it is as if it acquired a greater weight. The energy is drawn from the Synchronic Lines passing through that point by utilising the Synchronic Knots, the Minor Lines, and the passage of energies.

131

In the Temples of Humankind we can measure and verify changes that have taken place in whatever comes into contact with the Lines: by looking at data systematically, for example, differences in temperature and humidity are noted. Moreover, by studying a square kilometre of territory to observe the evidence of phenomena, one could discover the direction of the passing of the Synchronic Lines through a surfacing point.

Satellite surveys relating to sudden gravitational changes of the Earth have revealed gravitational jumps in several areas of Italy and Europe, including evidence of this around the town of Ivrea: we are looking at accentuated variations that induce transformations on the plane of form, it is, in short, as if forms here had a different density.

This means that an object in this area will be subject to a variation in weight, because in this vicinity the gravitational structure, as a temporal consequence, has had a modification to its mesh. One could conjecture that on this plane of reality there has been an energetic variation caused by the cabins in the Temples of Humankind[2].

Such cabins create a need to absorb a certain quantity of atoms from elsewhere to bring things back into equilibrium: as a result a sort of gravitational funnel is created. And the Synchronic Lines of course have their considerable influence in the manifestation of this phenomenon: a knot of Lines can cause jumps of even hundreds of metres in the orbits of the satellites passing directly overhead; the satellites that pass directly above this area are in fact subject to fluctuations in their orbit.

The Temples of Humankind are a great antenna as is their outer layer consisting of the Sacred Woods. In the past humanity followed surfacing points linked to the trees and the immense construction of Minor Lines existing in Europe has also been built in relation to the existing trees. In the Temples of Humankind the first incoming bend of the Minor Lines is situated on the altar in the Hall of Water: the access has an exact angle of entry and an exact depth. Starting from this initial angle there are another 130 fundamental bends which are a functioning part of the structure.

132

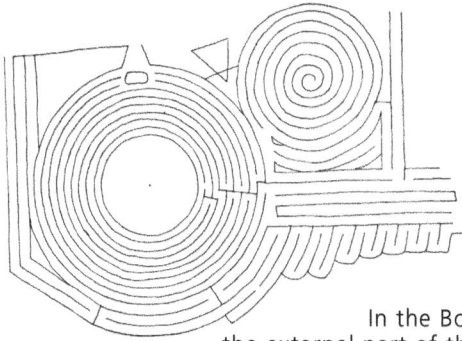

In the Bosco Sacro (Sacred Woods, the external part of the Temples of Humankind, miles of circuits have been marked out channelling and using Synchronic Lines energy.

In the mouths of the serpents depicted on the walls is contained the access formula for the Lines.

Some years ago a micro-passage was discovered which has been worked on to be able to make use of it at the right opportunity. It is possible to create much larger points of transit where even fair-sized objects can pass, thanks to an appropriate instrumentation and the labyrinth system.

The methods to accumulate energy are based upon the production and absorption of pre-selected energy. The energy is accumulated on a suitable structure of transformation and the Temples of Humankind constitutes precisely this, making use of the energy by multiplying it millions of times.

Since the Synchronic Lines are the vital system through which the complexity of our world circulates, not only does synchronicity flow down them but also a number of other energy streams which provide, for example, the possibility of transforming the energy of the time mines

133

in order to distil it, distribute it and increase its potential via the known systems.

It is possible to find thought forms concentrated in the energy of the time mines, in the condensing of the Synchronic Lines, in the densification of neutral events: this is a case of specific concentrations of various forms of possible uses of thought.

It therefore is not a matter of energy produced directly by human beings but it can be collected and manipulated. A peculiarity of this system relates to the torsion knot[3], formed by a stratification of events not expressed inside a time mine: this concentration of utilisable events represents a remarkable source of energy and even to stratify these unexpressed events it is necessary for there to be input from the Synchronic Lines.

134

[1] A Time Mine is a place where energy is collected – to later be manipulated and utilised – as well as neutral events, that is potential events not yet been utilised, which can be employed to operate on the structure of time.

[2] The Selfic Cabins are structures used for healing and for various experiments with space-time: their use involves the human physical and energetic structures, and thus the codes of the Lines reflected in the individual: the microlines. (See further the chapter on the microlines).

[3] Torsion knot: an object which contains complexity out of proportion to its mass-structure, with the capacity, therefore, to involve virtually other objects and to contain the sum of the data of other forms.

BETWEEN
PLANETS & GALAXIES

J ust as there is a map of the Synchronic Lines of the planet, a map could be drawn which shows the positions and designs formed by the lines that join all the planets of the galaxy.

Through these interplanetary Lines surges all the information regarding life developing on the individual planets. Therefore a being who incarnates from one planet to another will make use of this network as a road; in the same way, space travellers could use the synchronic channels for their movements using their subtle bodies.

The general forms of life that evolve on the different planets are influenced in a specific manner by the characteristics assumed by the Synchronic Lines. It is interesting to note that, around planets rich in life, the behaviour of the Lines is modified to a significant degree.

In future it will therefore be possible to discover where life is formed as well as the different types of creatures existing in the galaxy, thanks to the variation in the curvature of the Synchronic Lines in precise points of the universe. Where the presence of life in the universe is greatest the Synchronic Lines, linked as they are to the very formation of existence, form loops.

135

From what we may call the Universal Lines, that is those which join the planets and the different systems, the regional Lines spread out into the centres of life, as happens with the planet Earth. The moment a Universal Line touches the sun for example, it splits up into smaller lines that carry power and information to the sun itself.

Despite the movements of the planets, there exists a constant, continuous relationship between the Universal Lines and the planets. When an interplanetary Line brushes a planet, it divides up into a very large number of channels, which form a grid. The Lines, when they come across a planet, for example the Earth, are deviated and arrive at particular angle: almost a right angle.

136

The more synchronic Forces are split up, more possible it is to use them: by using the Minor Lines to vary their strength one can modulate input from the Major Lines - this is comparable to the energy of a flash of lightning which cannot be used to light up a small bulb. Given that life in its various forms tends to become identical on planets similar to one another, some kind of animal and plant life can be 'suggested' onto another planet.

When a form has been in existence for some time, and therefore ancient, it will as a result be highly evolved and will tend to spread itself throughout the universe and send its thought-forms onto other worlds. When a form evolves, it also makes use of symbiotic systems (for example human beings in symbiotic relationship with the trees, translator's note) to emit its own signals into space, which thus superimpose themselves onto those of other forms on the planet.

It is said: "Upon the Lines walk the gods" and, from what it seems, the galaxies are influenced by the Lines in a direct way: they have a tendency to shift and join up again right where synchronic knots are formed.

Thus, the shifting of the galaxies in the universe is orientated towards those places where, for all sorts of reasons, these Lines may gather density. In some places they intertwine transforming into veritable 'gateways' to other universes. Hence they create points of union, crossing points which are not black holes, though analogous in some ways. At these points it is possible to bring into contact universes on different vibrational, parallel planes.

Exchange between the various planets happens above all through the spiral form, which is the most widespread form of contact in this universe.

There are particular moments when what we may call "windows" open, comparable to actual synchronic gate-ways which permit a passage into other worlds. Imagine a sun illuminating a series of disks rotating at different speeds and orbits around a central hub: at certain moments, on the basis of the disks as they are lining up that instant, a beam of light may manage to filter past them and reach the centre of the hub.

The probability that this beam finds its way past all the disks by chance is infinitesimal, while it could be greater if it were possible to regulate the speed of the disks through the Synchronic Lines, accelerating their rotation.

Through the use of these Forces it is possible to open doorways at will, so that the light gets through, and even physical objects. When that happens, the "seeds" of one world end up in another, which is why with the passing of time the different combinations of life are drawn outward on an ever wider scale. Imagine an open window through which the wind blows a handful of seeds, which will take root in the new world and grow and turn into plants.

In fact there is a constant reciprocal contamination between living forms: whether between the most simple or the most complex, the different forms of life tend to influence one another, which is why there is a relative stability inside the universe.

With the passing of time, newly arriving seeds have less and less effect because by now suitable life forms have been created in the place. The older and more highly evolved a form, the more easily it tends to spread throughout the universe. When a form evolves, it makes use of symbiotic systems to emit its own signals into space, which superimpose themselves onto those of other forms on the planet.

On planet Earth, for example, human beings make use of the trees as symbiotic forms: the trees live in symbiosis with us and constitute a bridge across which to emit signals inside the galaxy. These signals give information on the human species and other species.

THE SYNCHRONIC LINES
IN SPACE

All worlds are born out of chaos, disorder. By means of the Synchronic Lines and the distribution of intelligent orders, chaos is transformed into chance, i.e. the synchronic condition takes form which allows a much larger quantity of events to happen, including their specific laws.

The energy which flows through the Synchronic Lines is an infinitely greater power of the universe than that which binds atoms, infinitely greater than the electromagnetic force, or the force of gravity. The laws of synchronicity form the basis of all other laws.

141

The particles that spin around the atom do not collide with one another because they respond perfectly to the laws of synchronicity. In the same way, then, the threads which keep planets in their orbits could actually be Synchronic Lines, determining the balance between centrifugal and centripetal Forces.

We know Synchronic Lines are more intense where there is life. Accordingly a map showing the distribution of life in the universe could be reconstructed by mapping these Lines. All celestial bodies, all physical bodies, are in contact with this network. Where there is life however, these Lines broaden out into highways.

The greater the quantity and quality of life, the greater the width of these roads, and their density as they crowd together or thin out. Where there is a planet the Lines come together, entering and exiting at the poles. They form a single road with traffic both ways.

There are also great pulsating places within the galaxies known as "hearts", points of dimensional meeting between divine Forces and those of another kind. There are four such cross-over points in our galaxy which represent the hearts of the system. They relate to four levels or types of life, all completely different one from the other. As such, they are interdimensional gateways between the spiritual and the material, and act as fundamental pressure points which set these Forces in motion.

142

We have here to do with very intense life Forces which can exist solely because they find a channel within divine Forms. Here, life is projected onto matter, while normally the opposite happens. Thus, a reality of life is formed which, given such evolutionary conditions, leads into this other domain.

These hearts may not be violated, for if they did not exist the flow of life would cease and life could no longer appear anywhere. Hence they are defended and are maintained in equilibrium with each other. These are not realms that can be conquered one by the other - just as the liver does not fight with the heart or seek to dominate it. The Earth is not one of these hearts; life spreads all about and the present physical geographical placement of our planet is more of a strategic point at this moment.

The Lines are therefore streams of events with an orientation, sensitive to living forms, and by their nature carry a common message on the boundaries between very different species, so they are a kind of translator. The incoming signal may undergo refraction through the living species, perhaps involving very far away points on the planet, or points close to us.

These signals experience a maximum fluctuation during the solstices and equinoxes and are behind the messages of the trees to living forms in other very distant places following the Lines of life.

The Synchronic Lines we are specifically looking at in this volume are those of this planet, attributed to a time empire[1] based on time periods very far apart from each other. We know there is a time empire which we are closer to, compared to others, and now thanks to the Synchronic Lines there are links with it. At first we had no link with this time empire, resulting in our effectively being marooned in time.

A constant connection now exists but this has only been achieved very recently, after having established the first links with the temporal crossing points. The links have been achieved using fixed points of reference, for example the solstices – marked by the astrological clock – and by developing the technology of the cabins so as to construct from our point on the periph-

143

ery a kind of link with the great highways. What counts here is strategic location.

The knowledge and the utilisation of the Lines requires a technology capable of travelling in space and above all in time, since the management of the Lines has been the only element which has allowed one to get around the opening and subsequent closing of the above-mentioned space crossing points.

The Lines were not known as they are today to the colonisers of space and time but they were known to those who started controlled re-incarnation in various points beyond the space-time gateways. One of the fundamental gateways of the Synchronic Lines is situated close to our world, planet Earth.

144

As we repeatedly said, the Synchronic Lines abound where life is most concentrated: from these planets, systems as they are, linked to life, different forms of culture may be inseminated; these places can be diffusion points of universal knowledge. It is thus possible to influence culture, technology, science, and the very way of observing and perceiving reality.

At times technologies are rediscovered at a distance of millennia because they are "re-seeded": as if a bird flying through sensitive environments had left seeds of knowledge, discoveries, technologies, art, history, civilisation: dreams carrying information that a researcher could bring to fruition.

Thus knowledge and technologies of great import may bloom again.

Also, at a collective and individual level it is possible to increase the flow of thought: there are geographical areas that can channel a greater flow of energy, where White Clouds are to be found (see below, editor's note). The utilisation of selfs and selfic paintings, too, gives orientation to the currents, increasing these faculties.

The Space Monuments are another interesting reality, since they represent a mine of all the information realised by a civilisation. The creation of these space monuments in the universe has allowed for realities to be placed like rocks in the rivers, to increase the current in order to be able to invest more in a world or a region, at universe level.

The space monuments with these rich contents are programmed to stop at the most interesting systems of life. To input data into such monuments one makes special contact with the Synchronic Lines at an alchemical level.

145

[1] Time Empire: Time can be viewed as having a structure that unfolds in the material universe exactly like space, creating a territorial map that treats time like terrain

TRAVELLING THE UNIVERSE

As is clear by now, the Synchronic Lines are much older than the mountains they cross: we have seen that it is the mountains that are formed in accordance with the Lines and not the other way round.

It follows that if the planet Earth were due to disappear or explode or some other event of the kind were due to happen, on the basis of the economy of the universe, these Lines would slow down compared to the speed at which the planet spins on its axis, and then detach themselves altogether, and life on the planet would disappear. There would no longer be a law regulating the various functions and existences, which we call *chance* or *synchronicity*: this would bring about the destruction of the whole planet.

Cells would form that do not respect the harmonious laws of life: a very widespread cancer would be created which, rather than being an agent of order inside nature would, having wasted its vitality, be destructive.

Considering these conditions, there would no longer be any organised forms with sufficient density and a little by we should reach complete destruction. With the passing of time, there would be new configurations and developments, but they would be levelled out, because of the economy of the universe.

147

Every living species has the possibility of contacting the Synchronic Forces, the human species in particular could learn to realise journeys into the universe, at almost infinite speed, re-learning to do what it is said was done many centuries ago. Since the Synchronic Lines are the tracks, the ringing grooves, down which all kinds of information can be sent.

And the most "subtle" and finest way to travel could be to transfer one's consciousness from one point of space to another, to be hosted in a body different from one's own, perhaps on a far distant planet. Thanks to these antennae one can even travel beyond our universe, to communicate with other species. Having the right knowledge to modulate the Synchronic Lines, one could transmit messages and work on a planet without need of physical vehicle, or entry permits, to be there.

In fact it is much easier in the universe to trade in information and news than trade in physical objects, precisely because on the most disparate planets where life is generally similar, it can be relatively easy, having the right knowledge, to build any object whatsoever, it therefore becomes absurd to go on imagining a future where immense spacecraft carry huge cargos from one part of the universe to another: it is not necessary to transport matter, it is much more economical to carry information and build the desired object.

The Lines allow one to calculate and measure journeys into space: no other type of energy allows you to obtain information so easily.

148

As humanity begins to venture into the universe, we will be able to use the Lines to pinpoint the position of our own planet and the point we wish to reach. To travel on the Synchronic Lines is to move in zero time, outside of time and space: you do not move along them in a linear way, but by bending space.

Travelling on the Synchronic Lines, you might come across anything and everything and so that fear becomes a form of defence. Suitable points for transfer have been identified for years, natural places or ones made suitable thanks to spheres and selfic equipment: it is a case of transits that remain open for a certain time before closing again. Some of the people who have vanished mysteriously, may have done so precisely after entering these gateways.

149

There are valves in time and space which open and close such doors, which in some cases may open in later times in the same place or nearby; these points always have a connection with the Synchronic Lines.

One can also imagine that the famous figures at Nazca might have been ritual circuits which, when walked down at the right pace, gave access to space-time gateways. The great labyrinths of the past in fact might have constituted points of transit from one universe to another, from one world to another, from one earth to another.

It appears that there are even gateways between different points on the same planet: following the Synchronic Lines it could therefore be possible to walk a ritual design in such a way as to move almost instantaneously from one point to another of the planet.

The Synchronic Lines in space are the roads of life, since they bring into contact the places where life is in some way compatible.

150

The Nazca Lines.

The Nazca Lines (designs) said to date from 300 BC and 500 AD, are geoglyphs, lines drawn on the ground in the Nazca Desert, an arid plateau that stretches for about fifty miles between the towns of Nazca and Palpa, in southern Peru. The more than 13,000 lines there form more than 800 figures, including stylized representations of animals common in the area. The lines are drawn by removing the stones containing iron oxides from the surface of the desert, revealing the undelying gravel which is lighter in colour.

WHITE LINES OR
WHITE CLOUDS

In addition to the Synchronic Lines, there are many other such roads of the living Earth, like for example the White Lines. These are islands of influence which are systems in movement, they move as if there were oil slicks on water, with their own times and own pace, each one with a different function.

The White Lines or White Clouds are currents and they only appear to be lines, or rather they give the impression of flat, floating hanks of wool, attracted by the concentration of life. They move almost like streams of cloud, they roll around, are pushed away or pulled close by currents of emotions.

151

We call them White Clouds because they take on every useful colour decided on by whoever manages to control them. They are made of one of the eight kinds of non-substance-substance (NSS) and their natural fluctuation is a cycle of around eight years. At times similar flows of White Lines overlap as if there were a cycle of four years.

They act like cloud systems, very slow in their movement: when they stop over a territory, in some cases for decades, not to say centuries, they encourage the development of civilisations, and then events take place that would not have happened in other times.

Like green grass springing up after steady rains there would be artistic development, and profound social and political changes.

It is possible to draw forecast maps of changes and what could happen by studying the movement of such currents, just as we might make a map for the movement of the clouds. If it were to rain for a long time over desert land, it would bloom and grow.

You can predict but not direct their movement, which is why they can be marked on a map, in order to know where they will be stationed for several years. Like any cloud formation, they can shift to different places; their course takes about eighty years to then return to their places of origin.

152

The White Lines flow on the planet and are mobile (while as we know the Synchronic Lines are more or less static and it is the Earth that moves).

They pass by and where they go they change the way of thinking and looking at events on the part of every living form: for this reason they are used by divine or para-divine Forms, to modify the way living creatures feel, influencing specific regions; they also have the function of regulating the currents of emotions these Forces feed on.

The White Lines have their importance as regards the intensity and the direction of feeling: they can give it a direction, attenuate it or moderate it.

Just as one can be sensitive to the weather and hence influenced by atmospheric conditions, so one can be influenced, perhaps deeply so, by the presence of such Lines.

Normally these Lines go through us, changing the way of thinking about things and re-organising memories, modifying them and transforming motivations. The personal identity of each person – thought inalterable – is thus transformed, given a direction, programmed, independently of what one thinks is happening.

The ways of thinking, the orientation of the mass of individuals (revolutionary, social, political…) are therefore in good part influenced over a cycle of eight years by the Force of these Lines, influencing fashions, tastes, styles, the sense of what is beautiful and ugly in a given period. Art on the other hand is not touched by these streams of energy, since when it really is art, it constitutes a much broader reference than that represented by this influence.

153

In the economy of the universe these Lines serve to change the direction of the behaviour of *animals en masses*, they change instinctive behaviour allowing single groups or individuals to assert themselves. They are the driving Force for the evolution of reactive behaviour.

The places touched by this Force modify the flow of time, producing strange phenomena that can be made use of: for example the use of these Lines allows retroactive modifications to be made in the memory of individuals with the aim of changing their way of thinking, to change the course of logical or illogical, emotional or rational actions.

The White Lines have an important material function because they break up the static nature of things, the tendency to look at events according to a given repetitive template, cutting through and allowing new ways of seeing reality to open up.

For animal species adopting certain patterns of behaviour over millennia, the possibility of changes of this kind is essential for survival: if the world were to change suddenly and such animal species had no history of environmental innovation, they would be easily destroyed.

Thus at times the arrival of these Lines can be important for their salvation: they change the direction of thought which otherwise would be consequential and purely logical.

154

They would seem to be brought about by the interaction of race minds, changing the evaluation of the archetypes of every species.

There can be smaller or larger Clouds which in any case have this cyclical flow. For example if they stop over Europe for a certain number of years or decades, economic, social and fashion innovations will be created more easily: what we have called the *Sources of the Nile*[1] are derived from these Clouds.

If you enter a Cloud of this type you can then know that the ways of thinking of the people in that area can change dramatically and if you find yourself at an access point for the Synchronic Lines it will also be possible, with the requisite knowledge, to give direction to the changes much more easily.

Even if (in a given case) it is not initially possible to know the changes, it is possible to influence them in certain cases: a change that can interest every living species or just one category, for example only insects, only flying creatures or only human beings. It depends on the signal, on the frequency of every life-bearing being: all living species are like radios that have a specific frequency.

A White Line interacts with human beings through the key points of the body's microlines, see below. It touches them and passes through, since the human density from an atomic point of view is nothing and the atoms of a solid object and of the void are the same.

These Forces pertain to nature and can be governed. It is possible to attract them with a commitment of months, years, decades, considering that they remain on a territory for a time that varies according to their breadth: if a Cloud is 600 miles wide and moves at a certain speed, it will take a certain calculable time to transit that zone.

Generally we are looking at long periods of time. And of streams of energy that have an orientation, fluctuating according to various angles. A Force which does not interact directly with inert matter but only with living matter, it is at the same time inside and on the surface. It moves in the spaces where the classic NSS, as we know it, might move.

The minimum time it takes for a white cloud to pass is around a few days. It is interesting to note that the thicker edges of these clouds can have different speeds.

As the fringes of a Cloud, these formations can break up, forming and re-forming even when they appear as a common front. They are more likely to stop over areas of the Synchronic Lines with particularly intense surfacing points.

[1] Sources of the Nile: sources of ideas that then develop elsewhere. (Author's note).

LABYRINTHS AND SYNCHRONIC LINES

E ven though the labyrinths[1] are formed from the Synchronic Lines, they are not the same since there is a fundamental difference: the Synchronic Lines carry the matrix of events, the labyrinths carry only the forms which manifest inside the events. Hence only at a few meeting points with the Lines can the opportunity arise for forms themselves to manifest.

The labyrinth network is superimposed upon the Lines but it is not on the same plane of existence and is not made of the same type of NSS. The labyrinth copies the circulation of the Lines: the interior will be experienced as infinitely confused form for anyone with no proper contact with the outside. It is as if two trains were passing one another other, and a passenger in one of the trains cannot tell if his train is moving or the other, there are no reference points.

You can enter the Labyrinth through the Minor Lines or through energy streams of that kind. If you want to enter matter you do not necessarily have to pass through the Labyrinth. There are points of contact between the Synchronic Lines and the Labyrinth, even if not all Minor Lines provide such a link. One of the reasons why churches and, earlier still, temples linked to the cult of death, were built at those points where the Lines come to the surface, has been the need to link the places of death and of life to the streams of energy that are the subject of this book. In any case the points of contact between the Synchronic Lines and the labyrinth vary greatly.

The Life form can enter into matter without being drawn into the labyrinth, however it is not a case of an automatic passage.

The life forms passing through gather experiences that then manifest inside the Synchronic Lines at the points of contact, and the race minds too can travel there.

It is possible to be contained by the labyrinth pattern without entering the labyrinth. If in the Synchronic Lines the events are neutral, events inside the labyrinth are very real conditions that can have contact with evolution.

It is not a question of a programme enabling you to do virtually anything at all but an opportunity con- structed over an immensely longer time scale which, being closer to a reality at the limit between the soul and the material realm, is an enabling Force, enabling experiences to be had.

For some it is actually essential to pass through the labyrinth. The fact that there are angles of entry or en- trances inside the labyrinth means that one can be cap- tured by it. Imagine you see open doors in front of you, you can take one and find yourself on the Lines, open another and you will enter the labyrinth, open still an- other and you will reincarnate.

If you enter a labyrinthine reality, you can develop a spiritual state or level compensating for what you might experience in life. The concept of labyrinth expressed here for some will mean Hell, for others Purgatory, for still others Paradise. Let us assume that it has three levels, three planes that indeed correspond to Hell, Purgatory and Heaven respectively.

Anyone who finds themselves on one of these planes cannot change it for another, since the labyrinth has planes inhabited by individuals destined to different realities. What distinguishes these planes? The type of current that runs through them is either a very negative current, a positive current, or both, positive mixed with negative.

It is as if events distributed themselves because attracted by some substance appropriate to them. The users will walk only on one plane or the other, but it is they who create Heaven or Hell: that is the type of substance it is ultimately composed of. Reality, after all, is formed according to the use we have made of the talents at our disposal.

We could also say that on the basis of the weighing of the soul, of its density, the soul ends up on one plane or another of the three. We might even imagine that persons with negative events become heavier and end up on the bottom. If and when they get lighter they begin to rise.

You can get out of this "hell"...either looking for a better one (!) with the physical body or looking for an opportunity for redemption, where this might be possible.

159

There are special exits which condition the user's reaction to eventual consequences: it is possible to return to the material world but bringing along a type of plan where you will be subjected to a flow of events appropriate to that concatenation, ones which make it possible to modify your position.

When one is outside the body time does not pass, when on the other hand one is in the labyrinth, time does exist. Even if time there does not have our valency, one has a vivid sense of the passing of what we call time.

You may find yourself in a situation like being in a film where you are walking along a corridor and going through a never-ending series of doors, one after another.

160

The mind in that form can imagine and interpret what exists around it: it does not see how things really are but how these are suggested by the senses. Colours there are not as we see them.

The Lines trace a kind of labyrinth where one can get lost during a wrong astral projection

In the labyrinth there are simply events happening. Whoever is able to condition them can move around; inside them situations can happen which put whoever is there to the test, but they will be able to overcome the various tests however: there is always the possibility of overcoming what is created as an obstacle by Forces hostile to humanity. There are other things we could say about labyrinths.

Anyone who is astrally projected and cannot manage to return to the point of departure will end up in a sort of labyrinth: this state of affairs happens when souls are not sufficiently refined to be able to leave the planet but at the same time they are not dense enough to be able to return; then they tend to enter and leave through different doors in a reality very similar to that of the labyrinth. This is one of the four fundamental types of labyrinth on the planet.

161

Another type of labyrinth forms a passage between worlds, There is a ferryman for souls from life to non-life and there is a ferryman for the opposite direction across the river of life, represented by a Synchronic Line with a tangent that leads out of the labyrinth one has entered.

Otherwise life would continue to flow inside the labyrinth in one of so many directions.

The formation of life to manifest in the material world must exit from here because only when virtual material enters the physical world can it really be organised and become living.

Life is organised on the information that it has managed to extract from the entirety of past lives. In other words, in this labyrinth of great complexity, to carry life as "Word" into material life, the vital impulse is needed and the ability to gather information on the infinite differences of life itself, so as to allow the development of evolution.

To return to the relationship between the labyrinth and the Synchronic Lines: tracing the network of horizontal and vertical Synchronic Lines, we see that a pattern of squares is formed. If we were to follow the Lines in these two main directions without heeding our twists and turns, the pattern we would describe would be a kind of labyrinth.

In practice, there is a division of the planet into meridians and parallels: these squares create a chessboard comparable to a labyrinth. The direction one takes can even be due to the influence of the Lines among themselves as one moves away or toward them. These then are circuits which, observed at a planetary level, divide up the planet in a somewhat similar way to the terrestrial islands on their smaller scale.

162

(1) Such labyrinths are formed by the Lines, but are not identical to them for one fundamental reason: the Synchronic Lines carry the matrices of events, labyrinths carry only the forms to be situated within events. Thus there are few meeting points with the Lines where opportunities can arise for forms themselves to emerge. Labyrinths have their natural manifestations in the continuous monitoring of conditions to adapt to virtually – since there is as yet no body through which form can find expression. They are roads that serve to secure an exchange of information not available to one during life.

SYNCHRONIC LINES, LAWS AND PROBABILITIES

D escribing the Lines, we have repeatedly mentioned several recurring patterns that they trace. There must be a connection here between a sequence of laws and the possibility of compressing and transforming what happens into dimensions apt for our surface reading.

Just as there are time mines in certain points, or concentrations of neutral (unused) events, one can imagine that in the case of the Synchronic Lines, constructions are also formed which could resemble what within the structures of time we call *time castles* or *loops*.

163

But they belong to two different situations. This phenomenon can be explained only with a rather special use of the time matrix relating to the functions of the Lines. Every law that governs the universe has its matrix. Synchronicity is one of these laws and has a matrix.

The functions of the matrix in some way become the connection point between the laws and the functions of the Lines. So here we are looking at something very different from what we have hitherto considered: we evaluate the Synchronic Lines from the standpoint of our species: they are linked to the concept of repetition of phenomena.

If there were an ideal surfacing point of this particular current able to influence things beyond the level of cause and effect but without for that reason being read as a purely synchronic function, then what we would have would be a point of diffusion of elements linked to probability.

This theoretical particle (posited here) would clarify the connection between the laws of the infinitely large and the infinitely small, meaning in this case the connection between the laws of the quantum microscopic level and the macroscopic level, making clear what can happen in their interaction.

Notice that every time an odd phenomenon happens with regard to the macroscopic laws, one ends up considering the laws of probability and as a result one has recourse to the laws of quantum physics which make use of chance. It is in fact chance that a particle can be in one place rather than another.

However, that chance circumstance has a precise way of manifesting, according to the laws of probability. It is true that every time dice are thrown, the probabilities that the same numbers come up is theoretically the same – since each throw has nothing to do with the previous ones. However, in reality the law of probability cuts in, which sees to it that the numbers that come up are distributed evenly.

With regard to the similar patterns that the Lines repeatedly make, there are no corresponding similarities in the fractals, instead these patterns (which we have to draw in

164

two dimensions) have to do with the potential of the Lines for carrying out functions with an increase or diminution in synchronic events.

Synchronicity is a current. Inside the Lines the current divides into two different streams, which may have different speeds. This means different amounts of the diffusion of possible events per moment, which can be read as probable events.

There is a greater quantity of elements towards the centre of the Line, sparser towards the rim, with every convector movement you can imagine within these functions.

We have explained that proximity between the Lines is not a function of distance but is proportional to the events that can be brought together. In practice, the current is not equal everywhere. In one Line the Force of the current could be 10 while in another 45: they are still both Synchronic Lines but the effect is different.

165

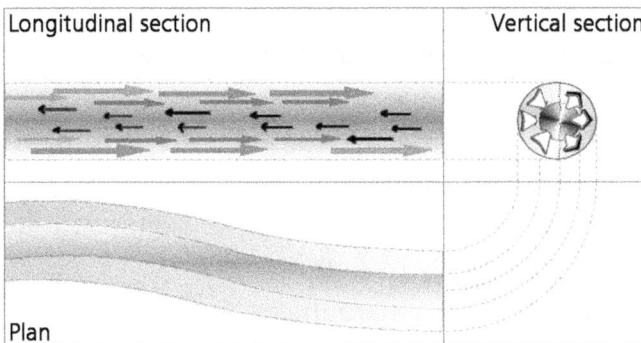

Distribution is not equal within the Line: there is a greater quantity of elements at the centre becoming sparser towards the rim.

Let us then bear in mind that on the same Line there can be points of greater density, stretches carrying massive synchronic currents and others with a much lower density (for instance points with values of 45, 20, 0, 10, 100 etc. on the same Line), with a minimal successive supra-connection with its precise value. Thus the value is not the same everywhere and can be different from that of other Lines.

Certainly the quantity and concentration of flow is greater where events having to do with synchronicity can manifest more: frequently these may be events related to physics, essential for complexity inside the system, or events relating to life, to the organic complexity which in its turn can have different levels. The greater the complexity of organic elements involved (an eco-system that manages to penetrate the spiritual) the greater is the possibility of influencing the Lines themselves.

For instance, a Minor Line could initially stem (depending on the directions needed at the time) only from the outside edge of the current, that being the energy that is needed. At a different time the area connected could be the central or core part of the current, where in theory there is a greater quantity and quality of current in terms of potential for influencing events whose direction lies outside of a theoretically balanced one.

Which means that if you are interested in an element that is synchronic for you it is more likely that you will manage it precisely because you want to use that faculty directing that something with the appropriate technol-

166

ogy – by using for example selfic structures or by using "repulsion systems": that is, there are systems that can make themselves impermeable so as to reflect Forces, deflecting them in other directions.

For example, when negative aspects are used or discharged, at times they can be used to create 'black mirrors' capable of deflecting a function which would become naturally "a-synchronic", because it would attract events where to obtain even the minimum effect one would need to expend the maximum of energy: hence a natural repulsion.

Compare being in an magnetic field with opposite polarity rejecting, deflecting or modifying functions. This kind of intervention is what we call Line surgery since in this case one can – literally – insert a by-pass.

167

So distribution is not equal over the whole of the Line but differs from point to point and in its turn is influenced by living aspects.

To give an example, in area where there is a forest and a great concentration of complexity and life, the currents that pass through that point will collect and carry many more convection movements than might be found in a desert. At times in fact the Oval Lines represent a usable surfacing which may lie at a great distance from where the Line is.

We are not talking here about a current distributing something, but a point of maximum probability of events according to the rules we have discussed. But it cannot be taken for granted that the Lines of currents follow on continuously, they could be discontinuous tracts but recognised as having the same value, as happens for example with horizontal Line C.

All this becomes even more salient at the points where these Lines plummet downward and do not then join up again, even if this does not always show up on the map. At the beginning of this research it was very hard to tell which line was which, when Lines resurfaced, or to identify the point where they changed their identity: for example where Line C becomes a vertical or north-south line: the research on these issues is much more complicated than it might seem.

THE MICROLINES

Considering the human being as the mirror of the universe, the microlines are like the atom compared to the sun: the human being is a dilatation of Forces, and is always, at all times, the exact copy of the universe. Our physical body corresponds to the universe of Forms, the subtle body to the realm of the "Threshold", the soul to the realm of the "Real".

As the Synchronic Lines join the Threshold to the other two zones, human beings are joined to their various parts through the microlines, roads that allow the subtle bodies – or the faculties that express them – to move according to the varying necessities.

The spiritual centre of everyone, which we call the soul, has thus a contact with the element which co-ordinates forms with the experience of matter.

We all have currents or lines which are exact copies of the Synchronic Lines: in the "little room" (the place inside of us where according to the ancient Egyptians we can find all the answers, author's note) within each person are all the roads forming a map of all one's own world and these roads are travelled according to one's abilities.

To do so means learning to dream, using the subtle bodies, acquiring knowledge.

169

The Synchronic Lines partake of the great rhythms and are a stable and fixed element: even this has a correspondence in the microlines, which reproduce the typical ebb and flow of the planet on the human body. Every eight years a particular pattern of density manifests which comes from the Synchronic Lines. There is a link within each person between their energies and those of the Lines.

In the microlines of the body there is a central vital point like that at the centre of the Earth. We see the macrocosm, the very plan of the universe, reproduced on a small scale in the human body. The surfacing points in this case are the *adonajaba* (chakras), which distribute the Force according to the greater or lesser pressure in these Lines.

Hence there are threads which can direct individual and collective choices: we are looking here at the common system which links life to life, which permits human thought to transit through the gateways of the Synchronic Lines.

For example the selfic cabins in the Temples of Humankind use bars which vibrate at a frequency appropriate to the various human components, to put the various key points of the individual in resonance according to the code of the Lines reflected on each person.

The microlines functioning in an individual are connected to the nearest points of the Synchronic Lines. The greater the complexity of the living being, the greater their proximity to a point of justice or stability, the more marked will be this ability to be linked like an antenna. By being close to access points to the Lines and knowing how to utilise the connection between the Lines and one's own microlines, one can increase one's individual power of knowledge.

The microlines cease to exist when the organism dies, just as there would be no more reason for the Synchronic Lines to exist if the planet were no longer there. Thus one can also draw a map of the microlines for the body. The microlines correspond to the energy Lines identified in the East in the study of acupuncture. That is, they are lines of energy, on the surface or internally, at different depths.

The lines on a globe then are like the network found in the body: rotating the globe, one notes fanning out and bunching. In the same way, the microlines touch various parts of the body and have points of maximum concentration at the tips of the fingers, the ears and the eyes. Thus there are points of maximum and minimum concentration on the body.

At times there can be a correspondence between the microlines and the *adonajba* (chakras). The *adonajba* are formed by the energies which course through the human being, but the energies travel first through the microlines and then through the chakras, which can be considered as work stations for the alchemy of living Forces.

Just as the lines of the planet do not cease at a certain point but go deeper inside the planet, so the microlines go inside the human being but run on continuously.

171

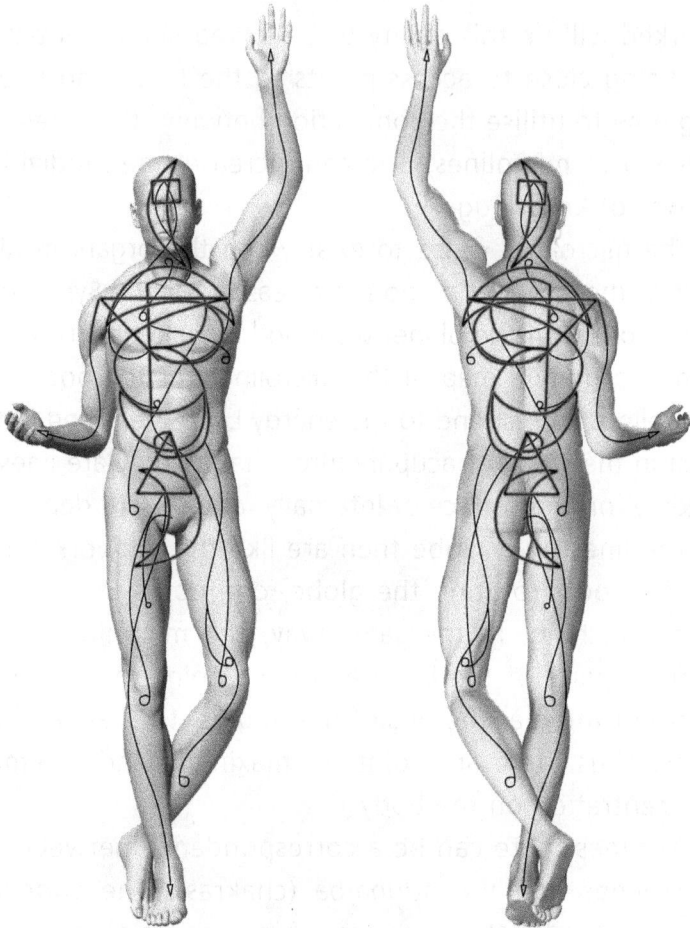

The microlines of the human body

They have their contact point with the major Lines out-side our dimension. Leaving aside the logic of Euclidean geometry for a moment, in order to understand the con-figuration we have to imagine that each of the micro-lines is exactly superimposed on the Lines of the planet.

Going beyond the dimension of the large and the small, one may imagine that two forms can be super-imposed even though they are on different scales: one reality can be the mirror of the other.

If we produce an event linked to a Synchronic Line that passes through South America, there will be a re-action at the corresponding point in the microlines of people in the vicinity. When one acts somewhere in the world, using the Lines, an intense correspondence is set up among the people who live in that place.

173

adonajba (chakras)

It is as if the corresponding section of their microlines becomes atrophied compared to the same microlines amongst people living elsewhere; from the map of the lines present in every individual and their intensity it is thus possible to determine the place of birth.

The current flowing along the microlines becomes particularly intense at points corresponding to the relevant geographical area.

The people who are natives of a place carry with them in their microlines specific characteristics and remain influenced by them even when they move far away. On the other hand, such people will receive the influences and information coming from the Synchronic Lines in their new location.

The microlines take on fixed positions which in certain moments fall outside the body when in certain postures, assuming a position in relation to the central axis of the navel that may even fall outside of the aura, the energetic field that surrounds all living beings.

These lines, in fact, unlike the immutable Synchronic Lines of the planet, have the characteristic of moving in a harmonious fashion according to the movements of the body.

Thus there are postures of the sacred dance[1] that mean your assuming positions ideal for the microlines: in fact the microlines move at a different rate from the body, often going before it: in any case, thought itself is faster than the physical action which follows from it.

When a person moves swiftly, they leave a trail behind them. The movement of the microlines is normally coordinated with the body – generally moving ahead of the body itself, like an acceleration of the movement, although under some other conditions it may fall behind.

The movements of the sacred dance follow the positions of the Lines: in this way the body-temple works at making contact with its own microlines: by assuming a natural position with awareness, contacts across several points are opened up, permitting the maintenance and reception of increased energies.

To find a suitable rhythm one may also assume yoga positions to physically bring together and harmonise points, making signs with the body, so to speak writing with it. Indeed, the positions of the Damanhurian discipline known as Meditative Harmonisation could help the re-balancing of the microlines; these are positions which have the function of joining together specific energetic points of the body creating a circuit.

There are positions which in their three-dimensional magical design formed by the human body have a significant symbolic-ritual importance. This is feasible only with living beings, by means of which it is possible to produce resonant effects. It would be difficult, on the other hand, to physically gather up and bring together two points of the planet!

Over a period of 70 days the micro lines change and evolve to then return to their starting positions, and every detail of the lines returns back to where it had been.

175

It is thus possible to observe a fluctuation and a successive re-positioning at the same points. In this way we can identify in advance the configuration of the microlines in relation to the body's central axis and to predict the position for each day.

Through specific positions that operate on the microlines it is thus possible to set the *adonajba* (chakras) in resonance as the point of contact between individuals: when this type of contact happens ritually one can have a reciprocal resonance between the masculine and feminine which is symbolically expressed as the androgyne where individual choices can profoundly change one's subtle format.

176

When one is in an inharmonious environment, the auras and the microlines become reduced or stalled. What is alive can live only in the midst of what is living, while this cannot happen in the midst of what is not alive: this means that it is easier to recover the lost movement of the mind and body in nature: the microlines find a more natural rhythm in woodland than on a concrete platform.

If one loses the rhythm of life, even the microlines lose their harmony and so vitality ebbs. The microlines are not composed of the non-substance substance but rather of life Force, vital energy.

The microlines of all human beings are the same, although they can be more or less active on the basis of variables such as the intensity of choices or whether the environment where one is has greater or lesser vitality.

They are to scale, with invidual colours, changing in response to conditions, all in proportion to the life form that hosts them.

And when that life form dies the microlines dissolve and disperse, no longer having any reason to exist.

Not just human beings have microlines: other living beings do as well; even if the forms are different the Lines are always alike, the body must therefore adjust more quickly than the microlines can. They represent the contact with the kind of life Force on this planet corresponding to the beings that live on it.

Events can be influenced because there is a correspondence in all beings: the magic of correspondence which works on the principle that like responds to like. The microlines sustain the interaction of events, since we are immersed in a river of time.

Inside this stream of time which in many cases curls back upon itself, each person is conditioned by the world and at the same time influences it: there exists a continual interaction between the living Forces, which are necessary to maintain the existence of life.

Thus if these Lines were to weaken one could die from loss of vitality: it would mean leaving the river of life, the flow of possible events. These Lines influence events, they serve to produce events and sustain the possibility of making choices. Just as they themselves receive.

The microlines are inherited soon after the foetus begins to form, several weeks after conception and represent the scaffolding of the physical body.

New ones are formed with every new birth, no matter what microlines the person had previously: a complete new form emerges whose depth is drawn in time.

During our lives we leave a sort of magnetic trail wherever we go, which is more or less dense according to the intensity of the directionality impressed on events.

Just as a distant event produced on a Synchronic Line influences a specific point on everyone's microlines, so every act of individual free will produces events which will have a corresponding effect on the whole planet.

The microlines allow events to manifest through us, passing from the Synchronic Lines. They carry out actions of correspondence, they serve to make events move. The Synchronic Selfs can serve to interact with events.

The personal synchronic selfs generally reproduce the map of the microlines taken from the Synchronic Lines. Pranotherapy, on the other hand, does not produce an effect on events but on the body and on the mind. It does not heal through the microlines.

The divinities are linked to the use of the microlines, at their level they have the possibility of drawing power from them and influencing life from the Lines of life. Just as the Synchronic Lines can be freed, so it can also happen with the microlines: this is what is called enlightenment.

Symbolically, if an enlightened person frees his or her own microlines by correspondence this takes on such power as to supply this resonance to everyone else who can then more or less make use of the opportunity according to their own free will. Plants, too, have their specific microlines, like all species.

But trees are often cut down before reaching maturity. Every plant has its own microlines and possesses a kind of intelligence that will increase with its penetration in time, proportionate to the length of its life.

A tree begins to have a certain weight, a certain value – able to be a powerful antenna, with appropriate potentiality and intelligence – when it has a large enough extension and it roots have spread out for at least ten metres (30 feet) from the bole, so as to connect with the outgrowths of other trees.

Undergrowth, and all natural territory in fact, is one big nervous system of enormous breadth and extension. And every place offers new things to our inspection, like a botanist strolling through woodland. Around every place, too, there reigns a forest, a forest of the subtle world, not easily explored, and full of mysteries. So, for example, there will be subtle forests where forests once existed – vanished only according to the river of time in which we are immersed in this material world. Energetic traces remain, though weakened by a thousand factors, by Oval Lines, by Minor Lines and so forth.

Places inhabited for thousands of years have over time reacted, developing in the ecosystem a precise relationship with human beings not only at a physical level but also at a subtle level: in every area there are manifested different somatic traits, habits, rhythms and traditions of life, but specific passages are also activated on the microlines in a less perceptible form.

For this reason if people who were born in different places far apart, get together they are able to compose more complex patterns of synchronic microlines.

[1] Sacred dance: An art practised in Damanhur, It is "based on the Magic principle of like attracts like, through which it is possible to recall and restore the archetypes". Via Horusiana, (Falco).

JOURNEY ALONG THE SYNCHRONIC LINES TO THE CENTRE OF THE EARTH

From the writings of Falco Tarassaco (Oberto Airaudi)

T he account that follows is the stuff of pure science fiction – no matter: I shall tell you about it all the same.[1]

According the studies I have carried out, several horizontal Blue Lines, those that seem to flow around the world forever in endless loops, may have a special function in addition to the very significant characteristics already discussed.

181

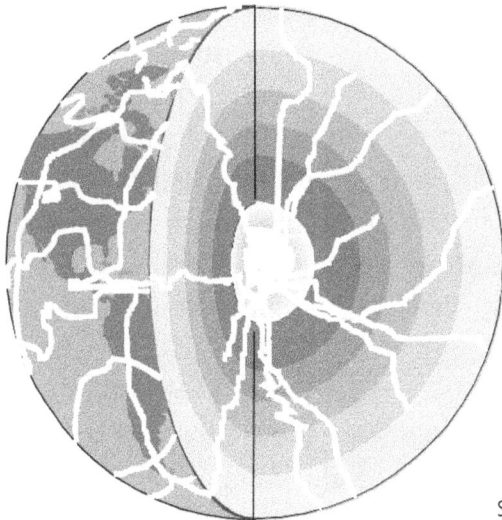

Section of the
lines inside the Earth.

In particular we are looking at Lines D-E-F, which, as you will remember, plunge downward at a certain point, toward the centre of the globe.

Their only companion among the vertical Lines is the Seventh, which similarly turns downward toward the Earth's core close to where Line F does the same.

In the course of my life I have tried for a long time to solve the mystery by taking advantage of the golden energy of several Minor Lines, to be able to travel on them astrally projected thanks also to a certain personal experience in this field.

In the end I tracked this down in one of the great "libraries" of the human race mind (i.e. a locale where all the experiences of the human race are gathered, author's note) where I found traces of very ancient visitors, travellers who came to this planet when the surface of the earth was very different.

So I made a journey to the nether regions, being able to follow Line F to the "end of the line". To do so, as I physically approached horizontal Line E near the equator, I made use of a specific magical programme and was able to trigger a line which I would describe as calm. I then took the plunge and like a boat on a river (remember Charon?) I floated along selecting the eastbound stream.

After swiftly crossing Africa, and part of the Indian Ocean, I drew on energy from a minor source in Ceylon, which I had made ready two and a half years previously, when I physically visited the spot.

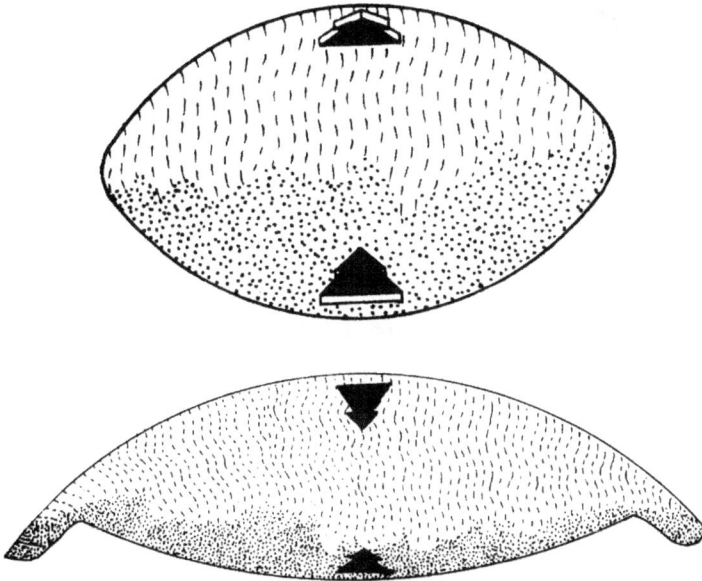

Section of Synchronic Lines with streams. 183

The combination of what I can describe as "synchronic-energetic thrusts" allowed me to turn and slip into the southbound stream of the Seventh vertical Line.

From this point on, it was all new even to me.

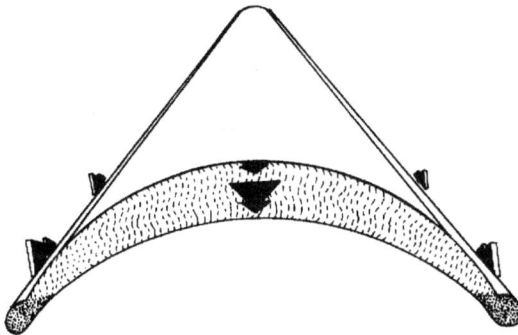

Section of Synchronic Lines showing opposing streams.

I prepared everything in order to travel exactly on the limit bordering the stream going in the opposite direction, so as to be able to do a swift U-turn at any moment.

I shall pass over all the adventurous incidents of this very special kind of journey to get to the important bit, the crux of the matter.

At a certain point the Seventh Line actually meets Line F. And I transferred over onto it. Line F appears hugely flattened and slightly curved, as does the Seventh Line.

As one travels downward, its shape tends to widen far beyond 900 metres to 2,500 metres (2,300 yards) the maximum flattening so far.

Furthermore, the lower, or return flow (see diagram), at a certain point splits into two distinct branches, located at either outside edge and slightly swollen.

184

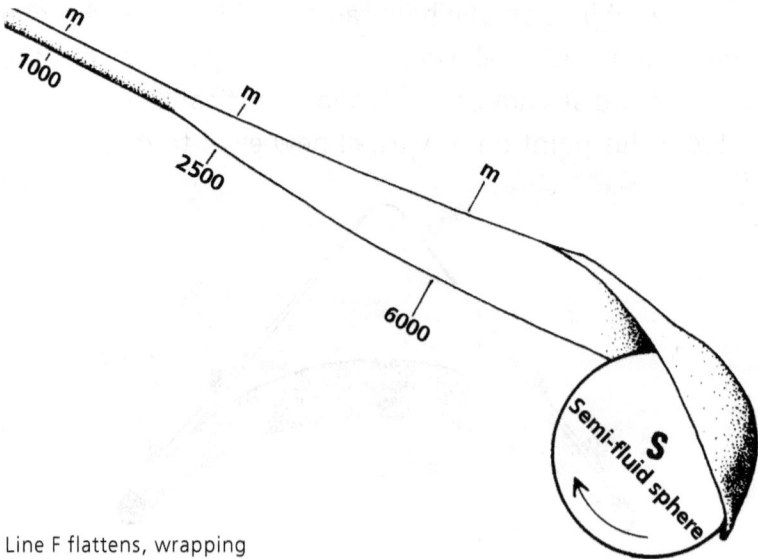

Line F flattens, wrapping
around the semi-fluid sphere.

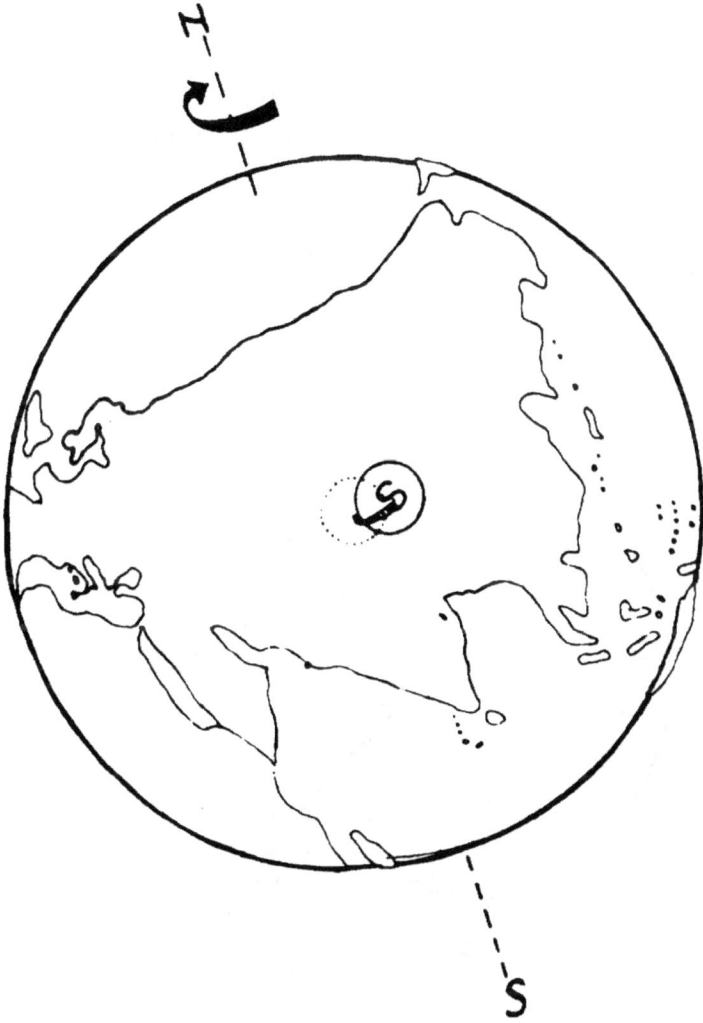

185

Semi-fluid sphere, not aligned
with the centre of the Earth.

Meanwhile the descent towards the centre of the earth was becoming more pronounced. And here is the interesting discovery.

Suddenly the mass I am crossing begins to move to the side, and Line F follows the new direction almost at a right angle.

We are looking at a semi-fluid, but very dense sphere, which rotates out of phase with the Earth.

Their approximate arrangement is as follows:

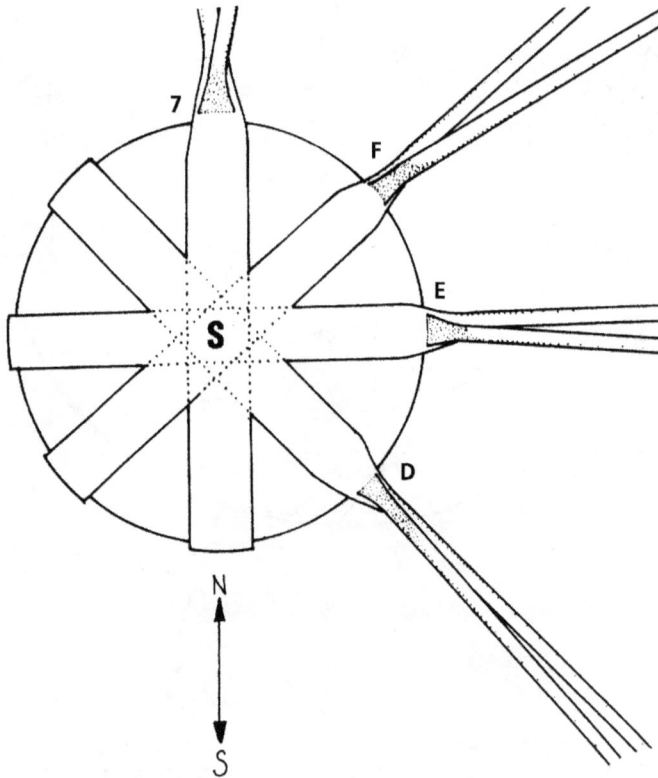

Lines D, E, F, and the Seventh envelop the
semi-fluid sphere for several layers.

Line F is wrapped around this sphere and ultimately flattened, so much so that it is transformed into just two dimensions.

Line F dilates a great many miles more, so that it wraps around this out-of-phase sphere, and twists as it does so. This twisting of the ribbon that is now Line F, transforms it into a kind of Moebius ring, in that the rotation of the sphere (actually slightly off-centre) causes it to meet up with itself again, intersecting with the other Lines several times.

This sphere is enveloped, like an onion, by several layers of ribbons coming and going, composed of the various Synchronic Lines: the vertical Seventh from North to South, and Lines D, E and F.

This all rotates about the Earth's axis faster than the Earth, thus taking less than twenty four hours to complete one rotation, and the Lines, having become two dimensional, wrap around themselves, crossing over several times, as if the other did not exist, until they detach again, as if due to centrifugal force, moving onto a plane further away from the central sphere and once more taking on the original tube-like shape.

Taking a look at a Line on its own, we notice that as it twists it dilates further, stretching out for dozens of miles. The flattened middle part keeps the two extremities connected: the outgoing stream keeps to one edge, by some means or other, while the incoming stream keeps to the other edge. I believe this is what happens: that this central sphere is shared with other parallel Earths.

187

Centre of gravity

Phenomena of variations in
points of contact between
the lines and the sphere.

However that may be, it produces noticeable changes in
the Synchronic Lines. The latter, together with several
Minor Lines, spiral right into its centre.

From the surface of the
spheres Minor Lines penetrate,
spiralling, into its core.

This Force is sufficient to bend space beyond all limits; which means that at the centre we have a point (vaguely similar to the current idea of black holes) that compresses time and other dimensions.

LINE	COLOR	VALUE
D + E	Yellow	91
D + F	Yellow	91
D + 7	Yellow	91
D + E + F	Yellow	91
D + E + F + 7	Shining	365
E + F	Yellow	91
E + 7	Violet	24
E + F + 7	Golden	182
D + F + 7	Golden	182
D + E + 7	Golden	182
F + 7	Violet	24
		1414

189

Pressing onward from this point, the entrance to another universe will be found, contained inside this extremely compressed non-particle. In short, a Chinese box: inside the infinitely small, an entire universe, with the Synchronic Lines as the sole point of contact-origin in that they can be compressed to infinity.

I have not yet gone beyond this point but it is surely possible to access other directions and other spaces from there; probably it is a transition point for the Lines.

Which means that through this point a contact could be possible with another point, as if we were looking at a line of symmetry of one form in relation to another.

In fact there is not one single line that leaves one object (for example a microphone) and goes to an object on the table nearby (like a glass).

A distinct line of symmetry exists for every object, but lines of symmetry are in contact with one another by empathy.

One can imagine a similar phenomenon among planets able to host life; it is not necessary in this case that there should be a direct transition from one point to another, even though the external part of the Line exists which, after issuing from the poles of the Planet, has its connection, its road towards the nearest star. But quite apart from this, it is probable that we are looking at a gateway.

190

In fact one does not travel in a linear way down the Synchronic Lines, instead one moves by getting the right ticket and hoping to arrive at the right destination. Naturally, one then has to know who sells the tickets and where, and if they are tickets based on the distance or on the point of arrival or if they have any other special conditions. As we have said, one travels by bending space, which is the dimension that interests us. If for example the space to travel was a table cloth and one wanted to go from one point to another, it would be more convenient to, so to speak, fold the cloth so as to make the two distant points touch rather than go on a straight-line journey to the distant point.

Returning to the discussion about the interior of the Earth, the extraordinary shape taken by the Synchronic

Lines around the inner core of the planet needs to be emphasised.

These orbits are not regular but jump from lower planes, almost touching the sphere, to higher planes, like for example the parts of the Synchronic Lines which break surface on the planet: D-E-F and 7.

When they run on the Earth's surface these Lines take varied forms, loops and angles. However, when they move into the inner orbits, as they approach the central sphere these tubular "channels" become "ribbons", becoming more and more regular.

191

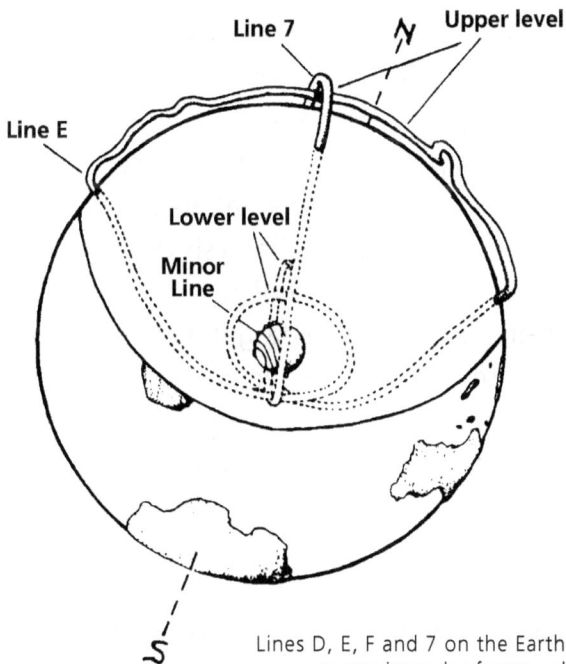

Lines D, E, F and 7 on the Earth's surface assume irregular forms, while when approaching the Earth's centre they become more and more regular.

The Lines can be travelled down even when they be-come two dimensional precisely because they are not to be considered in terms of their volume: instead imagine them as ultra-subtle rail tracks running side by side, go-ing in opposite directions. We put forward the Moebius ring as a reference: a shape which develops on one plane but which then appears to become three dimensional, which is why one can follow it in two opposite directions along each side of its shape.

The fact that the Lines can be distinguished even when they reach the centre of the Earth, is due to the fact that each Line has its own characteristics as if they were different colours: imagine a ball of wool made up of dif-ferent colours, the colour can be recognised even when looking at it from different points.

192

Perception happens not with the five senses we normally think of, but with the use of what we call the inner senses, which allow us to clearly distinguish the different aspects.

The sphere at the centre of the Earth is used because inside every world there is a gateway to other levels of worlds where matter has special laws, especially if there is life around. Such laws are put to a special use inside the Earth. As we have seen, we can imagine this ener-getic point which is not exactly on the axis but slightly shifted or eccentric.

Here we enter a point of time-space completely differ-ent from ours, both in the flow of time, and in the or-ganisation of matter. If there are portals, there must be translation points that physically we can regard as points of transition between different logics.

There are Lines that wind down into the interior of this planet by way of a complex route through a series of internal circuits; this is a very complicated network that is also connected to the Lines which issue from the poles.

Thus this information, these energies, do not only arrive on Earth through the gateways at the poles, they also come through this central point inside the Earth: this is both an exit point and an entry point. The vital Force exits from points identified with the poles, according to the distribution of the Lines.

Different realities can come in and be distributed from the centre of the Earth, in the same way in which they come in from external surface points on the planet. Let us take the Lines inside the planet as having thickness, while considering those crossing the galaxy as two dimensional. Where there is a warp, there is a weft: hence the vertical alignment as opposed to the horizontal one, can be seen to be arriving and departing from that point.

The centre of the Earth is not a point that can be conquered. It is the only road intended and imagined as the entry and exit for the Force known as the *Grail* and which, in the material spaces considered here, is both vertical and horizontal: no other Force is able to use this doorway.

Out in the galaxy, beyond the planet Earth, there are few other points as important.

193

[1] What follows tells of a personal experience of Falco Tarassaco

MAPS
OF THE SYNCHRONIC LINES

THE SYNCHRONIC LINES
OF PLANET EARTH

A B C D E F G H I = 237.000 km. circa

1 2 3 4 5 6 7 8 9 = 177.000 km. circa

6   7 8   9

A

B

C

D

MARIANNE

E

MARSHALL

SALOMONE

MALDIVE

FIGI

NUOVA CALEDONIA

G

MAURITIUS

7

TASMANIA

H

ISOLE KERGUELEN

6   8   9

LENINGRADO

MOSCA

Minsk

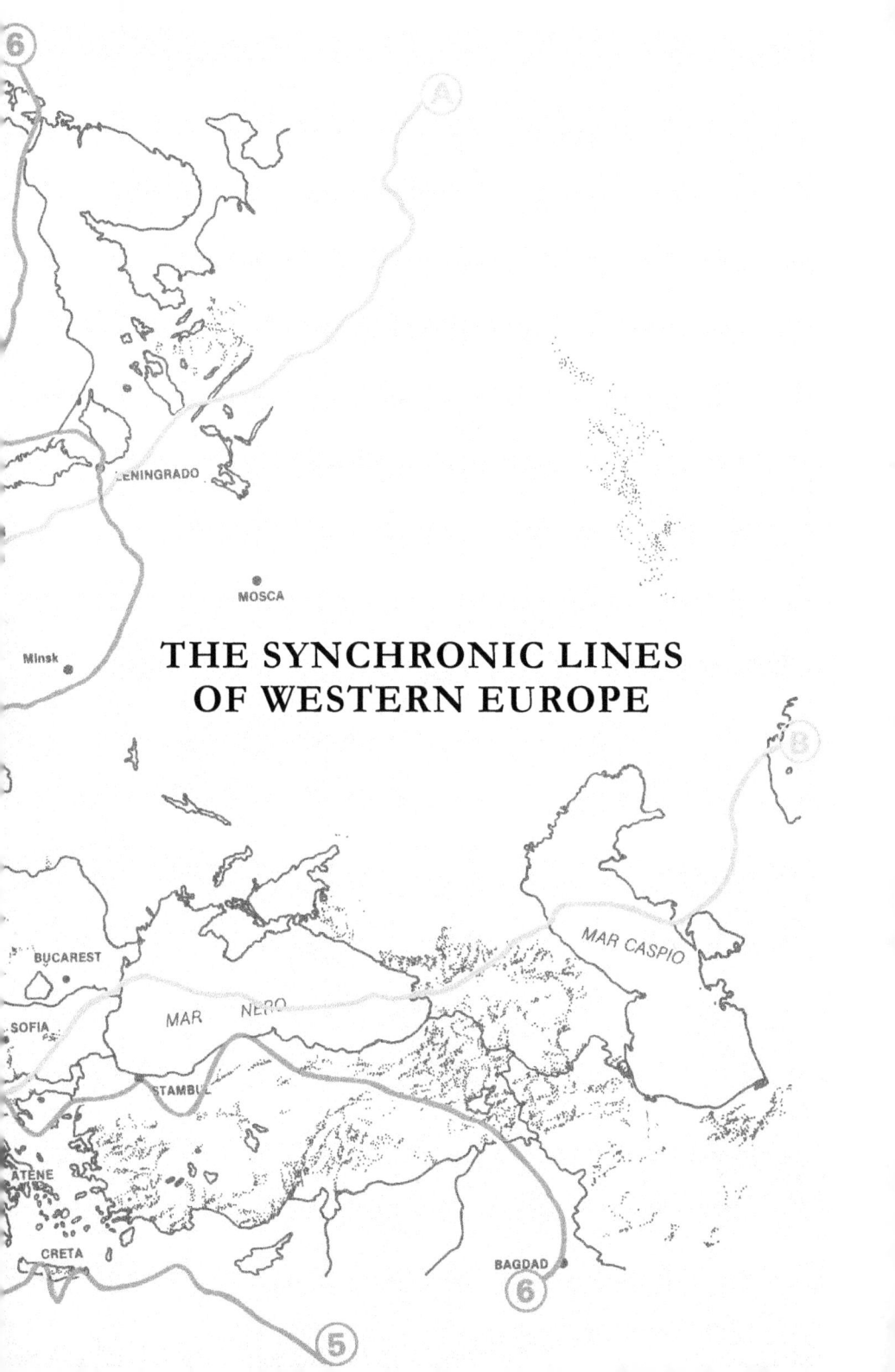

THE SYNCHRONIC LINES
OF WESTERN EUROPE

BUCAREST

SOFIA

MAR   NERO

MAR CASPIO

STAMBUL

ATENE

CRETA

BAGDAD

THE SYNCHRONIC LINES
OF NORTHERN ITALY

A

MONTE ROSA

MONTE BIANCO

AOSTA

BIELLA

DAMANHUR   IVREA

VERCELLI

VIGEVANO

PAVIA

VALLE DI SUSA   TORINO

ASTI

PIACENZA

B

ALESSANDRIA

ALBA

CUNEO

COLLE DI TENDA

MAR LIGURE

CAP FERRAT

Olbia, Messina, Istanbul, Bagdad

6

5

Praga

Linz. Praga. Varsavia.

VETTA D'ITALIA

A

6

PASSO MONTE CROCE

BOLZANO •

TRENTO

CAMPIONE

DESENZANO DEL GARDA

MARE ADRIATICO

• PARMA

BOLOGNA

E DELLE RADICI

MONTE CIMONE

PISTOIA

FIRENZE

B

5

Perugia, Mar Nero   Malta, Creta

THE SYNCHRONIC LINES
OF ITALY

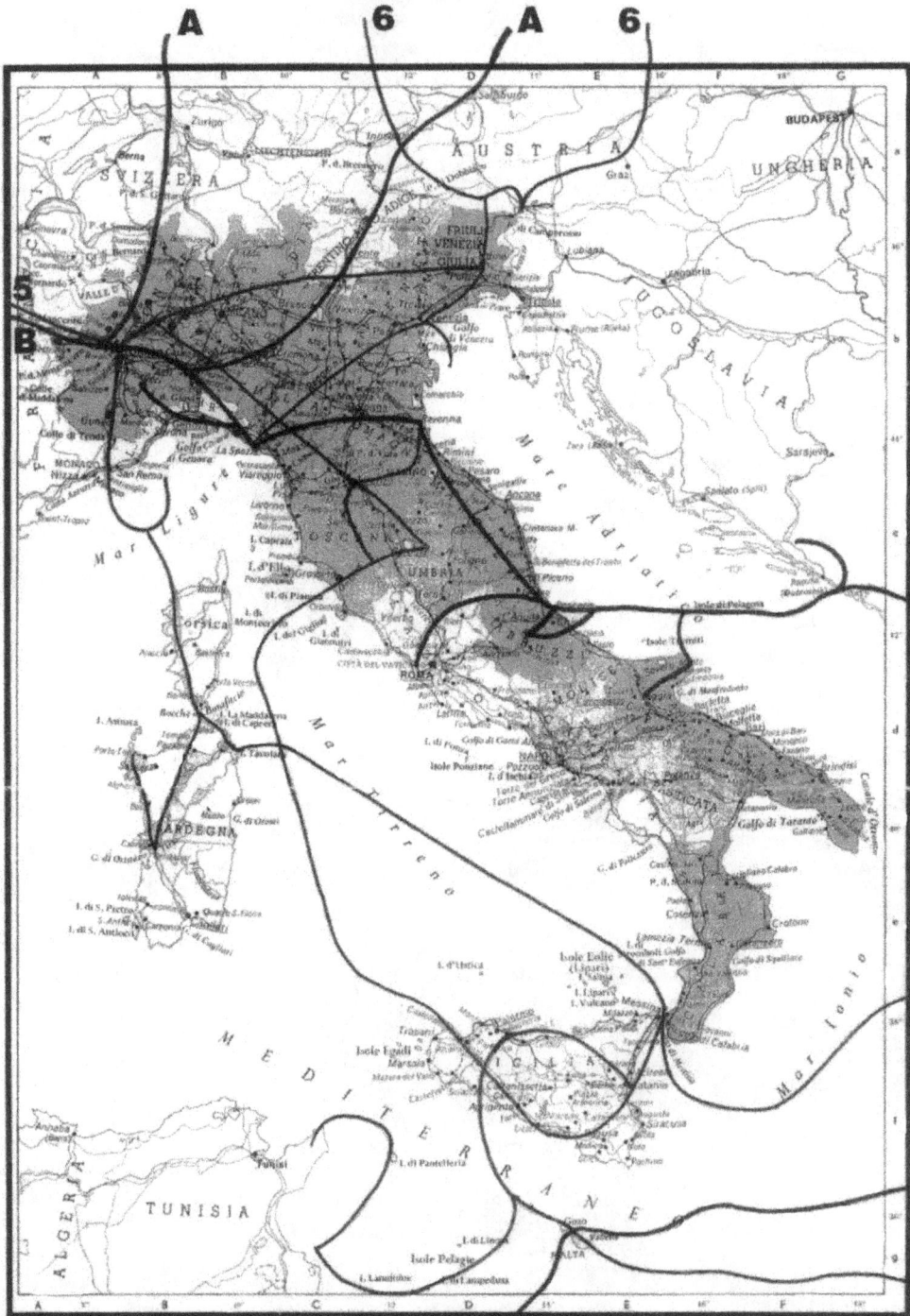

Scala 1:5 000 000